ARCHAEOLOGY OF NIHOA
AND NECKER ISLANDS

The Bulletin of the Bernice P. Bishop Museum (ISSN 0005-9439) was begun in 1922 as a series of monographs presenting the results of research in many scientific fields throughout the Pacific. Beginning in 1987 the Bulletins continued with a slightly modified title as four new series: Bishop Museum Bulletins in Anthropology (ISSN 0893-3111), Bishop Museum Bulletins in Botany (ISSN 0893-3146), Bishop Museum Bulletins in Entomology (ISSN 0893-3146), and Bishop Museum Bulletins in Zoology (ISSN 0893-312X). Each series is sequentially numbered, beginning with number 1. Bulletins are issued irregularly.

Bishop Museum Bulletin in Anthropology 9

ARCHAEOLOGY OF NIHOA AND NECKER ISLANDS

BY

KENNETH P. EMORY

BERNICE P. BISHOP MUSEUM

BULLETIN 53

TANAGER EXPEDITION

PUBLICATION NUMBER 5

MUTUAL PUBLISHING   BISHOP MUSEUM PRESS

First Printing, October 2002
1 2 3 4 5 6 7 8 9

Mutual Publishing
1215 Center Street, Suite 210
Honolulu, Hawai'i 96816
Ph: (808) 732-1709
Fax: (808) 734-4094
e-mail: mutual@lava.net
www.mutualpublishing.com

Bishop Museum Press
1525 Bernice Street
Honolulu, Hawai'i 96817
Ph: (808) 848-4135
Fax: (808) 841-8969
email: press@bishopmuseum.org

Printed in Australia

FOREWORD

Nihoa and Necker are two islands that mark the transition from the high islands in the southeastern part of the Hawaiian archipelago to the atolls scattered throughout the northwestern part of the archipelago. Hawaiian oral traditions and the archaeological record indicate that these islands were the northwestern frontier of the lands populated by Polynesians who first settled the archipelago.

Nihoa and Necker were apparently uninhabited at the time of their "rediscovery" by European navigators in the late 18th century. However, evidence of a prior occupation of both islands covered the landscape. Both house and agricultural terraces were discovered on Nihoa and numerous platforms and heiau type structures were found on Necker. The 1923 and 1924 Tanager Expeditions were organized, in part, to record cultural sites and collect archaeological specimens from Nihoa and Necker.

This publication is a re-print of Bernice P. Bishop Bulletin 53, authored by Kenneth P. Emory and published by the Museum in 1928. The contents are based on the notes, maps, photographs, and specimens collected during the Tanager Expeditions. The Bulletin is being re-printed in order to provide a baseline of 20th century knowledge regarding the archaeology and ethnology of Nihoa and Necker.

The cultural interpretations included in the original Bulletin did not incorporate the Native Hawaiian voice or traditional ways of knowing as a means of understanding the evidence of the material culture that was left behind when the last inhabitants departed the islands. By re-printing this publication, the Museum is providing 21st century scholars with the opportunity to re-interpret the data collected by Dr. Emory almost eighty years ago. More importantly, it provides an opportunity for Native Hawaiian researchers and cultural experts to approach the information from a point of view that is guided by the traditional and contemporary practices of their culture.

William Y. Brown
President and CEO
Bishop Museum

CONTENTS

ILLUSTRATIONS

Archaeology of Nihoa and Necker Islands

By Kenneth P. Emory

INTRODUCTION

Nihoa Island lies 150 miles west-northwest of Kauai, the nearest of the inhabited Hawaiian islands; Necker Island lies another 150 miles to the westward. Beyond Necker, the westward trend of the Hawaiian chain is extended by a number of volcanic remnants, sand islands, reefs, and shoals, all widely separated. (See map, fig. 1.) Both Nihoa and Necker are volcanic islands less than a mile in length, rising steeply from the sea. They are sparsely covered with grass and shrubs and are frequented by thousands of birds.

The historic Hawaiians were apparently unaware of the existence of Necker Island. When Nihoa was discovered in 1789, it was uninhabited and unknown to the Hawaiians save through tradition. In 1857, house terraces were discovered on Nihoa; and in 1894, stone images and rows of upright stones placed on platforms were found on Necker. Although a number of visits were made between the time of discovery and the year 1923, no ruins had been recorded, and the images, utensils, and implements collected without data were insufficient to determine who these early occupants were or why they were there, except that some early culture, differing markedly in some respects from the known Hawaiian culture, was represented. Accordingly, when the Tanager Expedition (19, pp. 19-24; 20, pp. 19, 20)[1] was organized in 1923, one of the main objects was to record the ruins and collect archaeological specimens on Nihoa and Necker, and also to search for traces of prehistoric visits on the rocks and sand islands to the northwest. The work was planned with the hope that a comprehensive and detailed survey would make it possible to ascertain the cultural relationships of the archaeological remains and thus lift some of the obscuring mist enveloping the beginnings of the Hawaiians, and the early peopling of Polynesia.

On the islands to the northwest of Necker, no evidence of former occupation was found by the Tanager Expedition, but on Nihoa and Necker the ruins were extensive and fortunately little disturbed by earlier visitors.

---

[1] Figures in parentheses refer to the Literature Cited, page 123.

This report is based on the notes, maps, and specimens resulting from the Tanager Expedition, and on fragmentary material previously obtained by Bernice P. Bishop Museum. Almost all of the few specimens previously removed are available for study. I have endeavored to here record all the ruins on the two islands and to describe all the archaeological specimens collected, revealing the ruins and specimens in their proper setting. I feel confident that little if anything of importance has escaped notice. An attempt has been made to define the cultural position of the islands with reference to the main Hawaiian group and to Polynesia as a whole.

During the visits of the *Tanager* in 1923, the archaeological investigation was conducted under the general direction of Bruce Cartwright, Jr., who spent six days (June 12-15, 21, and 27) on Necker, and five days (June 16-20) on Nihoa, assisted at various times by Mr. Edwin L. Caum, Mr. A. L. C. Atkinson, Mr. William G. Anderson, Charles S. Judd, and other members of the field party. The survey on the two islands was completed under my direction during the last trip of the *Tanager,* July, 1924. I was ably assisted by Mr. Kenneth I. Hanson, Mr. William G. Anderson, Mr. William Bush, Mr. George Kimball, Mr. Theodore Dranga, and Mr. A. Landgraf, and from time to time by Dr. Harold S. Palmer, Dr. Erling Christophersen, and sailors from the *Tanager.*

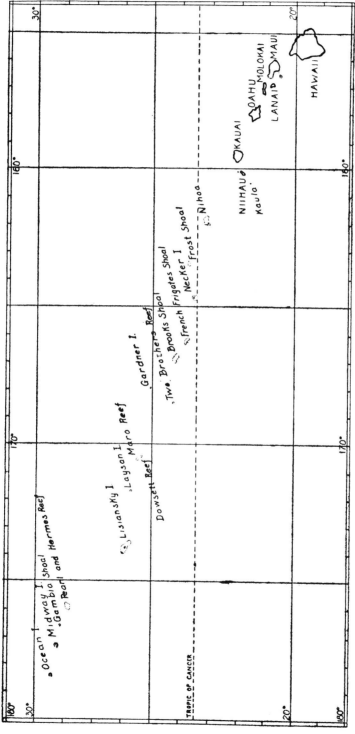

FIGURE 1.—Map of the Hawaiian islands.

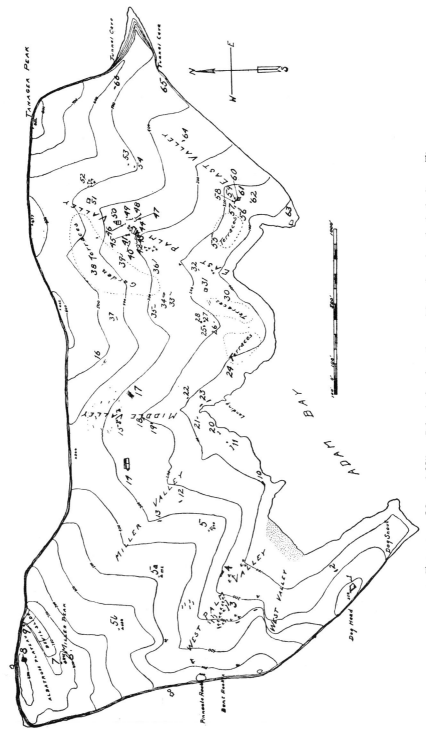

FIGURE 2.—Map of Nihoa Island showing the position of archaeological sites. The ruins are located, oriented, drawn to scale and numbered consecutively from west to east. Contour interval 100 feet. (Topography by Charles S. Judd.)

NIHOA ISLAND

GEOGRAPHY

The little volcanic island of Nihoa lies 150 miles from its nearest neighbors, Niihau and Kauai at the southeast, and Necker Island at the northwest. The island is plainly visible at a great distance, and approached from either east or west appears as a great rock tooth. It is nearly a mile long and averages about one-quarter of a mile in width. On the north it rises in a sheer cliff three-quarters of a mile long, 350 feet high in the middle and a little over 850 feet high at each end. On the east and west inaccessible cliffs meet the north cliff roughly at right angles. The land on the south sloping steeply down to low bluffs bordering the wide Adam Bay is cut by six small hanging valleys. A wave-washed ledge, 10 to 50 feet wide, except for several small breaks, extends around the bay at the foot of bluffs 50 to 100 feet high and accessible in many places. While rarely a landing may be effected in the westernmost cove of the bay on a small sand beach, the east ledges of the middle cove afford a safe landing much of the year. (See fig. 2.)

Nihoa comprises 156 acres, but the level or gently sloping ground is less than half that amount. All slopes are covered with several varieties of grass; weeds, saltbush, pigweed, and dock are plentiful in more sheltered places, as are also *ilima, ohai,* and a number of other shrubs. The only trees are 515 *loulu* palms (*Pritchardia remota*) of which there are two large groves, one in East Palm Valley, and a larger one with 347 trees in West Palm Valley. The hau, hala, and coconut are lacking, as also all other plants and trees which were most important in the daily life of the Hawaiians. Judging from the vegetation, Palmer (37, p. 10, 15) estimates the rainfall as 20 to 30 inches a year. He describes the springs as follows:

Three small seeps were observed, all of them at the bottoms of streamways. They represent ground water which is held up by relatively impervious layers of basalt, or which circulates through fissures in the basalt. The smallest seep is a little west of the head of the middle cove, and issues from crevices in the cliff behind the terrace. The second is at 270 feet elevation in the large valley to the east, and appears to have been the source of supply for the former inhabitants who left numerous rock platforms and terraces in this neighborhood. The water here appears to be brought out of the overlying soil and rock by a massive and relatively impervious lava flow. The largest discharge of water is by seepage from the conglomerate body at the head of the west cove, and is brought to the surface in the same way. The water of all these seeps is heavily charged with acrid-tasting matter, presumably derived from the dejecta of the multitudinous birds and is nitrogenous and phosphatic in character. It is so strong that it seems impossible that the natives could have become accustomed to it, but no other source of water supply was found though all of the *Tanager* party were on the lookout for seeps and springs.

Nihoa teems with bird life, nearly every foot of the island is covered by birds, and, day and night, the air is filled with them. The birds noted by the Tanager Expedition included five kinds of terns, three kinds of boobies, Bulwer petril, black-footed albatross, Nihoa finch, Nihoa miller bird, wedge-tailed shearwater, tropic bird, and frigate bird.

Seals occasionally are found on the island. Turtles are fairly common, and Adam Bay abounds in fish. Lobsters, crabs, and shell fish may be collected on the wave cut terraces of the coast.

HISTORY

At three o'clock on the morning of March 19, 1789, Captain Douglas of the *Iphigenia* discovered Nihoa, and hove to until daylight to obtain a good view of the island. Mears (34, pp. 359, 360) writes:

This island, or rock, bears the form of a saddle, high at each end, and low in the middle. To the south it is covered with verdure; but on the north, west, and east sides it is a barren rock, perpendicularly steep, and does not appear to be accessible but to the feathery race, with which it abounds. It was therefore named Bird Island.

Corney (11, p. 73) in the bark *Columbia,* with 60 native Hawaiians on board, passed Nihoa on April 17, 1817:

Next day we passed Mokoo Manoo, or Bird Island. There are no inhabitants here although the land seems good and covered with coconuts and plantains.[2]

On information gained from the Journal of Captain Alexander Adams (47, pp. 66-74), Thrum (48, p. 7) bases the statement that the island of Nihoa, known to her generation only through tradition, was sought for by Queen Kaahumanu in 1822, found and annexed to the Hawaiian domain in that year.

A translation of an account of this visit written by the native historian, S. M. Kamakau (27) follows:

While Kaahumanu was dwelling on Kauai, the idea came to her to search for Nihoa, a land not seen by the generation of her time, but found in the stories and songs of the old people. Perhaps Kaahumanu had listened to Kawela Mahunaalii:

Ea mai ana ke ao ua o Kona,	The rain cloud of the south comes,
Ea mai ana ma Niho-a,	Comes from Nihoa,
Ma ka mole mai o Lehua,	From beyond Lehua,
Ua iho a pulu ke kahakai.	Rain has flooded the beach.

In the mele of Hiiaka:

Ea mai ana ma Nihoa,	Comes from Nihoa,
Ma ka mole mai o Lehua.	From beyond Lehua.

---

[2] Mokoo Manoo (Moku Manu) is of course a literal translation into native of the name, Bird Island, given by Captain Douglas. Corney evidently from his distance mistook the *Pritchardia* for coconuts and plantains.

Thus, there were many chants and prophesies, making known all the lands of Kahiki.

Therefore, the thought of sailing in search of Nihoa became fixed in the mind of Kaahumanu. "Say, children, let us sail in search of Nihoa." Kaumualii [her husband] agreed. Two or three boats were prepared to sail. William Sumner was the captain, and also the leader, and Nihoa was found and it was annexed to the Hawaiian Group.

In 1857 King Kamehameha IV landed to formally annex the island to the Hawaiian Kingdom. The log of Captain Paty (36), of the Hawaiian schooner *Manuokawai,* describes the visit. The third paragraph of the following extract is taken from Captain Paty's original log written in pencil. The other paragraphs are from his official log book, given to the Hawaiian Government.

Wednesday 22nd. [April] Nearly calm all day. At 5 p. m. got within 5 miles of the island. Sent the boats in to sound . . . Lay off and on during the night.

Thursday 23rd. At 6 a. m. descried a sail to the eastward, which proved to be *H. Imp. M.S. Eurydice.* At 8½ a. m. came to anchor . . . at 9½ took letters on board the French man of war ship, for His Majesty, Governor Kekuanaoa, and His Excellency, Mr. Young.

At 10 a. m. went ashore (got upset in landing). The King and Governor landed at the same time in a canoe . . . a small drain of water was found near the landing but I believe it impregnated with sulphur. About a dozen seal were found on the beach and the King shot several of them.

I deposited a bottle at the foot of the pole near the landing place, containing notes agreeable to my instructions . . . also a plate of copper on which I scratched 23rd April A. D. 1857. King Kamehameha IV visited this Island, and took Possession.

Not seeing anything to warrant my longer stay here, I got under way at 3 p. m. At the same time the French ship of war filled away, with His Majesty and friends on board, for Honolulu.

The "Polynesian" (38, May 2, 1857) contains the following regarding the King's visit to Nihoa:

The *Eurydice* has been absent 16 days, effecting a landing on Niihoa and brought away two of the inhabitants,—sea lions,—one of which is still . . . alive. . . . From the description given the island is quite a pleasant spot, covered with grass and shrubs, some low trees of the fan-palm species, known by the natives as *loulu,* and occupied by birds out of number.

According to the "Polynesian" (38, Feb. 12, 1859), the U. S. Survey schooner *Fennimore Cooper,* Lieut. John M. Brooke, commanding, sailed from Honolulu December 29, 1858, on a cruise lasting until February 5, 1859, to ascertain the exact position of the many islands and shoals lying to the northward and westward of the Hawaiian group. Careful surveys were made of Bird Island, Necker Island, French Frigates Shoal, Gardners Island, Maro Reef, and Laysan Island. From the records in the Public Archives and local newspapers I can learn nothing further of Lieut. Brooke's visit to Nihoa and Necker.

In 1885, the steamer *Iwalani* was run on an excursion from Honolulu and Kauai to Nihoa. Sereno E. Bishop accompanied the excursion to make such topographic surveys and geologic observations as circumstances permitted, in behalf of the Hawaiian Kingdom. Sanford B. Dole served as ornithologist, a Mr. Jaeger, as botanist, and Mrs. E. M. Beckley as representative of the Hawaiian Government Museum. The party was composed principally of H. R. H. Princess Liliuokalani and friends, and over 200 other excursionists, mostly Hawaiians. Bishop and his assistants landed in the first boat about 8:30 a. m., on Wednesday, July 22, 1885, near or at the "landing" marked on the map (fig. 2).

Bishop (7, pp. 3-4) states:

Ascending the cliff some forty feet with difficulty, we came out upon the steep slopes. These were well covered with sweet bunch grass known as makuikui. . . . Portions were thickly covered with *ilima* or *sida,* and other small bushes. Two small groves of palm trees were conspicuous, the chief one in the large eastern valley, the other in the central one. . . . Two stations were chosen for a base line, one about 200 feet inland on the most central ridge at the height of 207 feet [within a few feet of Site 26], the other across the large cove on the brow of the cliff, 126 feet high. The latter station was upon a ruined terrace of stones [Site 10], probably one of several house foundations which the very accurate Dr. Baldwin informs me that Kamehameha III found on Nihoa, being not far from the best landing and the chief water hole. . . . [Kamehameha III was only 8 or 9 years old at the time of Kaahumanu's visit to Nihoa, in 1822, and had died several years before the visit of Kamehameha IV, in 1857. Either "Kamehameha III" is a mistake for Kamehameha IV, which is probable, or there has been an expedition to Nihoa of which no record exists.]

We were proceeding to occupy a third station . . . and expecting two hours more work whereby to establish our survey by the help of many flags set up by Mr. Rowell on lofty points, when a fire broke out about 300 feet above my main station [Site 10], and spread with great speed and force in the mass of dry tindery matter. This at once filled the island with such volumes of smoke that it became impossible to measure any angle on any flag. The last of the hundreds of people who had landed had already disappeared below the cliffs, and were slowly embarking. We reluctantly retired from our work and followed them. Within an hour my station had been swept by the flames which spread steadily in every direction.

The embarkation was much more difficult and hazardous than the landing, the sea having risen somewhat, as well as the tide. Two boats had been swamped, one of them causing the loss of most of the negatives taken on shore, and the destruction of the cameras, Mr. [W. E. H. Deverill] Deverell saving his own life by extreme activity and strength.

What may have been lost in the overturning of the boat it not known, but Princess Liliuokalani brought back the stone bowl shown in Plate XVII, *C.* A stone dish (Pl. XIX, *A*), coral rubbing stone (Pl. XV, *A*), and coral file (fig. 21), collected by Mr. Deverill are in the Bernice P. Bishop Museum.

In another account Bishop (6, p. 5) states:

The Princess and her train had landed and visited the palms, and were returning to the shore. The island had been ransacked for birds, skins, eggs, feathers. Over 200 people had landed and worked their sweet will. They were now beginning to go aboard, it being past noon. Doubtless there had been lunching and a good time.

A British boat, the *Hyacinth,* made soundings about Nihoa, in September of 1894, and a party may have landed at that time (35, Oct. 19, 1894).

Carl Elschner (15, p. 9) states that in May, 1910, several sailors of the *U. S. Revenue Cutter Thetis* swam ashore at Nihoa, and that Lieutenant Derby from the same cutter, and one sailor swam ashore to Nihoa in 1913 to secure specimens of rock.

The *Tanager* arrived off Nihoa the evening of June 10, 1923, and during the following ten days a topographic base map was made, eight sites of ruins recorded, and specimens including the finest of the stone bowls collected (Pl. XVII, *A*). In a cave not far from the landing, were found two soya tubs, a bottle of soya, decayed rice bags, and Japanese straw coats, where Japanese fishermen had been camping.

On Trip E the *Tanager* entered Adam Bay the morning of Wednesday, July 9, 1924. In the middle of the morning work was commenced at the lower bluff shelters in East Valley. (See map, fig. 2.) In the afternoon the clearing and measuring of the ruins in East Palm Valley was begun. On Thursday, July 10, the survey of the ruins in East Palm Valley was continued throughout the morning, and the excavations were greatly extended at the shelters in East Valley during the afternoon. On Friday, July 11, excavations were made in East Palm Valley, at Sites 36, 40, and 41. With the assistance of eight sailors provided by Commander King, the sites in East Palm Valley, and a section of the terraces at Site 24 were thoroughly cleared. Meanwhile the excavations at the lower shelters in East Valley were completed. A burial cave on Tanager Peak was discovered on Saturday, July 11, and the bluff shelter, Site 64. The last of the sites in East Palm Valley were mapped, measured, and photographed. In the afternoon, an important burial shelter, Site 2, freshly discovered, was carefully investigated, the ruin on the summit of Dog Head recorded, the lower part of West Palm Valley explored, and the sites along the southwest coast measured. Sunday morning, July 13, the bluff shelters in Middle Valley were excavated and all the sites recorded, as well as Site 14 on the flat between Middle Valley and Miller Valley. At noon the party embarked for Necker Island.

ARCHAEOLOGICAL REMAINS

GENERAL REMARKS

The gentler slopes of Nihoa are entirely stepped with cultivation terraces. The most level and sheltered spots are dotted with the ruins of house sites, and every suitable grotto gives ample evidence of occupation. Among the house sites are ceremonial structures consisting of conventionally arranged stone uprights. On the summits of the island are platforms strewn with coral heads which belie a nonutilitarian purpose. On high places and along ridges are a number of small stone enclosures appropriately called lookout stations or shelters. Of the two burial caves discovered, one contained bones of an adult male and of two infants, the other of four adults, one of them a female.

The once intensive cultivation of Nihoa, large number of dwellings and places of worship, the former presence of women and children, and the number and kind of the utensils, implements, and instruments left about the old abodes point to a time when the tiny island sustained a permanent or semi-permanent population. Were it possible always to distinguish between the garden terraces, house terraces, and ceremonial structures, an approximate census of Nihoa's maximum population could be formed. In my judgment at least 25 and not more than 35 of the larger terraces are house sites. There are 15 bluff shelters and not more than 15 ceremonial structures. Assuming all the bluff shelters and all the house sites to have been occupied at one time, and allowing five persons to each house site and three persons to each shelter, gives a population of 170 to 220. Going from one to another of the sites which appeared to be dwelling sites and attributing from one to eight persons to each site, according to the number which suggested itself to me as most suitable, I arrived at the figure 174 as the highest possible number. However, it strains my credulity to believe that more than a hundred people ever lived on Nihoa. Approximately 12 acres were under terrace cultivation, or 7.7 per cent of the total area (156 acres) of the island. Presumably the main crop was sweet potatoes. The average yield of sweet potatoes at the Hawaiian Agricultural Experiment Station in Honolulu (8, p. 9), based on tests covering five years, is four tons per acre.

If the 12 acres of terraces on Nihoa produced 48 tons a year, a little less than 1,000 pounds a year could be supplied to each of a hundred individuals, and this amount would be only a meager supply. Fish, birds, and bird eggs were to be had in abundance, but the water supply must have been a serious drawback to the increase of the population or their prolonged stay on the island. In fact, the means by which they obtained enough water to exist is a mystery. Only three small seeps were discovered and the water from all of these was so tinctured with the leachings from guano as to be as unpalatable as salt water.

RELIGIOUS STRUCTURES

SMALL ALTARS

Fifteen ruins on Nihoa seem to have had some religious significance inasmuch as they possess certain features not common to dwelling sites, shelters, or garden terraces, but which features are associated with some religious structures in Polynesia. They include cairns, terraces with uprights, and two unusual platforms. Because of their diversity and state of ruin, it is exceedingly difficult to form a clear picture of these structures.

Three small, crude, quadrangular and pentagonal platforms, upon which numerous coral heads and branches have been laid without order, stand on isolated prominences (Sites 6, 9, and 11). Upon two of the platforms lie several dike prisms which appear to have been placed in that position and not originally set upright.

Coral fragments were noted on two isolated, small, rough terraces on the coast (Sites 21 and 22). At the east end of the large terrace at Site 51 is a small, rectangular pavement with a cairn upon one corner. Coral heads have been set on the pavement and cairn. A number of coral heads were seen also at one or two corners of four other large structures (Sites 1, 10, 11, and 63). Undoubtedly the corals mark the spot where the rites employing their use were performed, but whether or not the entire structure was originally designed for these rites is uncertain, because each of these four structures differs from the other altars in possessing features which are characteristic of Necker Island maraes with which coral is not associated. It is therefore possible that the four structures are Necker or related maraes, where, subsequently, rites involving coral heads were performed upon a corner. The corner then would take the place of the small altars serving primarily for the coral rites.

TERRACES WITH UPRIGHTS

The terraces with uprights I interpret as sacred places although later investigations may prove that in terraces with only one or two isolated uprights, the uprights alone possessed a sacred character, or even that they served merely some utilitarian purpose. Certain it is that some of the terraces are places of worship because the order of their uprights is strikingly similar to that of religious structures elsewhere, but the uprights on some terraces do not have this order, on others they have no apparent order, and for terraces with only one or two uprights standing, it is uncertain whether additional uprights once stood upon them, and even where the presence of other uprights is indicated, their arrangement remains unknown. Enough survives of all the terraces with uprights to show that their grouping was not alike, in fact, that considerable variation existed among the most closely allied arrangements.

DIKE PRISM UPRIGHTS IN THREE ROWS

On four terraces (Sites 40, 41, 45, and 51) three fairly regular rows of dike prism uprights extend from one end to the other and a few uprights stand outside of this scheme. Practically all of these uprights are slender and tapering: the average height is two feet, and the space between them three feet. Some uprights are in pairs. Although every inch of surface of three of the above terraces was combed and partly excavated, no trace of their use as dwelling sites was found except a stone set on edge which might have been the side of a hearth at Site 40. The fourth terrace (Site 41) was littered with household objects. As this terrace was unquestionably a dwelling site, the function of the uprights presented a problem. If they were parts of the dwelling their only conceivable purpose would have been to support the covering. The middle row being of almost uniform height, 3 feet, and the outside rows approximately a foot less, the outline was suggested of a rectangular hut, 10 by 18 feet, shaped like a wall tent. A house 3 feet high and 3 feet between posts is somewhat incredible but not impossible. The uprights of Site 40, however, are not more than 2 feet high. To increase the height of the roof it is necessary to suppose that sticks were strapped to the uprights.

The only motive I can imagine for using dike prisms as supports for a house is the lack of timber. The native palm (*Pritchardia remota*) could have furnished good house posts as well as thatching, and, being a variety restricted to Nihoa, of course was present when the island was inhabited. Were the dike prisms parts of dwellings, it seems strange no shells, water-worn stones, or artifacts were found at Sites 40, 45, and 51, all of which were excavated.

It is my belief that the uprights have nothing to do with dwellings, and, that at Site 41, the uprights were erected for some nonutilitarian purpose, subsequently to its use as a dwelling site.

DIKE PRISM UPRIGHTS WITHOUT ORDER

At the rear of the small terrace, Site 28, are 7 dike prism uprights (fig. 7), of which the only suggestion of an orderly arrangement is the equal spacing of one row of three uprights. A single dike prism upright stands on the front and another on the back of Site 42, a house site. On the front of the third main terrace of Site 43, is a single upright. At the west end of a large terrace, Site 48, and near the front, is a single upright. Near the center of this structure is a small, dike slab upright.

ARRANGEMENTS OF DIKE SLAB UPRIGHTS

Back of the village in East Palm Valley, at Site 50, a series of terraces bear dike slab uprights conventionally arranged. The uppermost of these terraces is almost square. Along the rear is a row of uprights consisting of a pair of dike prisms in the middle and two dike slab uprights on each side. Before the middle uprights lies a stone slab, and further out on the terrace stands a single upright. (See Pl. VII, *B*.) On the right side of the un-paved terrace floor, two dike slab uprights, face inward; on the left side, near the rear and parallel to the rear uprights, stand a pair of slabs. Near the front left corner of the terrace floor are a pair of dike prism uprights and a single columnar upright.

The three terraces below the last undoubtedly form a unit. The upper-most terrace has a row of dike slab uprights, two standing on the left and two fallen on the right. The middle upright or uprights are missing. Against the middle front of the terrace is a single slab upright, and against the middle front of the terrace on which it stands is a pair of slab uprights. On the middle front of the lowermost terrace is a single slab upright. The right and left uprights on this terrace are arranged much the same as on the uppermost terrace.

Two terraces on the coast, Sites 10 and 11, each have two slab uprights standing parallel to the front retaining wall. The terrace, Site 10, is 28 feet long and 17 feet wide. A pair of firmly embedded dike slab uprights (Pl. I, *B*) stand at the east end and 9 feet from the front retaining wall. A very low, rough wall runs along the front and both sides of the terrace.

The terrace, Site 11, is 35 feet long and 7 feet wide, a single upright stands at one end and only 3 feet from the front retaining wall and a fallen (?) upright midway between the ends.

Coral heads were found on both terraces.

Site 63 is a large terrace sloping up to a stony rectangular area 12 feet long and about 6 feet wide. One or two low, thick uprights stand on this area; unfortunately their exact position was not recorded. A coral head and a dike stone, possibly a fallen upright, lay on the front left corner of the terrace.

A pair of dike slab uprights standing about in the center of the large terrace (Site 51) are aligned parallel to the ends and not, as in the median uprights of Site 50, parallel to the front or back of the terrace. It should be remembered that at the west end of this terrace is an arrangement of dike prism uprights and on the east end a small altar with coral heads. At this end also stand two slab uprights in the position shown in figure 15. There-fore, prominent features of all the structures so far discussed under the head of religious structures are present at this one terrace, indicating a religious structure combining the ideas back of all the others, or a successive occupation of the site.

RUINS AT SITE 1 AND SITE 8

Two probably religious structures not seeming to fit in with those so far described are the ruins at Site 1 and Site 8. At Site 1 the ruin consists of

a low wall, or narrow platform, 46 feet long, facing upon a considerable platform. Coral heads have been deposited on the extremities of the wall and
a dozen dike prisms, 2 to 4 feet long, have been laid across it at varying
intervals. From their position (Pl. II, *A*; fig. 3) I am confident that most
of the dike prisms could never have stood upright, on the other hand, I am
inclined to regard the four or more waterworn coral stone slabs fallen on
the outside of the wall or platform as originally uprights. Had they been
set on the wall this is where they would most likely have fallen, whereas,
had they been laid prone on the wall it is less likely that they would have
slid over while most of the longer, smoother dike prisms remained.

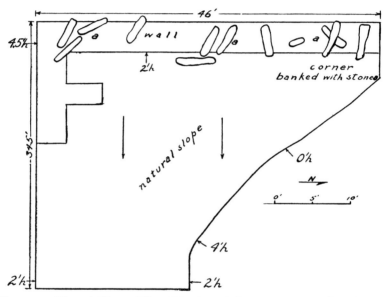

Figure 3.—Plan of Site 1, Nihoa Island: *a*, fallen dike prisms. 2′h, 4′h, and other
figures on the margins indicate height of wall.

The ruin at Site 8, on Albatross Plateau, is a low, comparatively wide
platform facing on a small enclosed court. Three short dike prism uprights
and two prone dike prisms are on the platform. Their position is shown in
figure 4. Another upright stands against the front right corner. No special
order is observable in the uprights.

HOUSE SITES

The bluff shelters of Nihoa scarcely could have contained all the inhabitants who built the 12 or more acres of agricultural terraces, and as palm
trees were available, it is reasonable to assume houses were built. Hence, I

assume that most of the large, well built, appropriately located terraces were house sites, such as, for example, Sites 34 and 43 (Pl. V, *B*). At some of these, a pavement of fine stones (Site 43), or a number of household implements (Site 42) indicate occupation. All these terraces are rectangular and have a floor on one level. Most of them are unpaved, but some are partly covered by a top dressing of rough stones, 1 to 2 inches in diameter. The retaining walls of the terraces are evenly faced and almost vertical. (See Pl. V.) The larger stones, especially those of the outer corners, are nearly of one size and have a flat, even face exposed in the wall. The interstices are filled with small, rough stones.

A hearth, consisting of three oblong stones set on edge and forming three sides of an 18 inch square chamber containing ashes and fine bits of charcoal, was excavated at the shelter, Site 19. At the neighboring shelter, Site 18, an earth oven was marked by some 25 vesicular pebbles mixed with charcoal. Windows made in the protecting walls erected at the entrance constitute a novel feature of three bluff shelters (Sites 18, 32, and 57).

AGRICULTURAL TERRACES

Most of the agricultural terraces are low, narrow, and long. The floors are rough and uneven, a characteristic most marked in the widest terraces. The retaining walls are faced with stones of all sizes carelessly laid up. (See Pl. VI, *A*.)

ARCHAEOLOGICAL SITES

In the following list archaeological sites on Nihoa are numbered consecutively from west to east, to correspond with the map (fig. 2) where each ruin is located and oriented, and drawn to scale. Their description includes only the information needed to supplement that to be derived from the map, the plans, figures, and plates. The plans of the sites are drawn to scale throughout.

Site 1. A rough platform (Pl. II, *A*, and fig. 3), maximum measurement 46 feet and 34.5 feet wide. Lies lengthwise on the crest of the ridge. A wall 4 feet thick, 2 to 4 feet high outside and 2 feet high inside, runs along the edge towards the sea cliff and encloses a third of the south end. The wall is built of large, irregular stones laid to form a nearly perpendicular face. Eleven or twelve dike prisms 2 to 4 feet long lie at irregular intervals along and across the top of the west wall; other prisms and at least four waterworn slabs of coral conglomerate, 5 by 10 by 20 inches, lie at the outside base of the wall. Several columns lie inside the wall. A large number of coral heads, identified by Dr. C. Montague Cooke, Jr., as *Pocillopora,* lie on the platform, particularly on top of the wall at the southwest corner.

In the southwest corner of the platform a shelter has been formed by extending a wall 5 feet long and 2 feet wide to the south wall and 4 feet from the west wall. The platform slopes steeply down to the eastern border, where it is 2 feet high. The northwest corner is banked with small stones and the surface of the platform is partly covered with a much disrupted pavement.

Site 2. Cliff burial. One of many recesses in the bluff on the east side of Dog Head produced by unequal weathering of horizontal beds of lava. On a shelf 4 to 8 feet wide, sheltered by an overhanging ledge 3 to 5 feet above it, were found bones of four adult individuals partly buried in dust and stones fallen from the roof of the cave. Four skulls lay together on a pillow of bunch grass (*Eragrotis variabilis*), 3 inches thick, and at their right and partly under the pillow were long bones placed neatly together. Directly under the grass and below the left skull were the pelvic bones of a female. In the dust below the skulls were a few other bones. (See pp. 49-50.)

Site 3. Terraces. Cooke reports terraces large enough for house sites, at the south edge and within the main palm grove of West Palm Valley. These terraces, he observed, are fewer, smaller and not as well preserved as those in East Palm Valley, and are much overgrown with shrubs. Just north of the palm grove Cooke saw several agricultural terraces of the form found elsewhere on the island. At the foot of the bluff above the palm grove are two caves, south one the larger and with a terraced floor. I explored West Palm Valley as far as Site 4, finding no other sites.

Site 4. Three caves with floors formed by a terrace. The northern cave is large enough for a man to sleep in. The terrace wall is about 5 feet high. Digging into the few inches of surface soil and partly removing the wall revealed no artifacts. The middle cave is a little larger than the northern one and slightly terraced. No objects were found in its two inches of soil. The southern cave is 9 feet long, 5 feet deep, and its platform extends 2 to 3 feet beyond the roof. On the floor of the platform was a basalt pebble. Complete excavation revealed no artifacts.

Site 5. Stone shelter (Pl. III, *A*), 5 by 5 feet on crest of a ridge. The walls of the enclosure are 2 feet wide and 1.5 feet high. An entrance 1 foot wide is located on the upper side. Recorded by Bruce Cartwright.

Sites 5a and 5b. Shelters similar to Site 5, having also the opening in the upper side. One of them is recorded by Cartwright as 5 by 5 feet (inside measurements) with walls 1 foot high and 1 foot thick.

Site 6. Platform on the rock ledge at the summit of Miller Peak. Quadrangular platform, roughly 6 feet wide by 9 feet long and 1 foot high. Two short, leaning stones (not basaltic columns) at the eastern rim of the platform might possibly be considered uprights. On the platform are scattered coral heads.

Site 7. A small natural bluff shelter at the back of which Caum found the jar illustrated in Plate XVII, *A*.

Site 8. Rectangular platform on level ground. It measures 9 by 18 feet and not more than 1 foot high. On the east is joined a rude enclosure 6 feet wide and partly open to the north. Three uprights of dike rock splinters and two fallen uprights are irregularly placed on the platform. The structure is much in ruin.

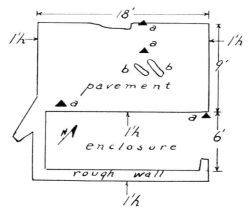

FIGURE 4.—Plan of Site 8, Nihoa Island: *a*, standing dike prisms; *b*, fallen dike prisms.

Site 9. A well built platform 6 feet square and 4 feet high. Laying on the center are 3 basaltic dike prisms and scattered over the top of the platforms are coral heads. Except for Site 6 this platform is on the highest point of the island. It rests against an outcrop of dike rock and faces northwest.

Site 10. A stone terrace facing the sea (Pl. I, *B*). On edge of bluff formed by a dike. The terrace is 28 feet long, and 17 feet wide, front wall 4 feet high, top of the front and side retaining walls 3 feet wide, a few inches higher than the unpaved interior of the terrace where stones and soil form a rough surface. Coral heads appear at several places on the wall and on the southwest corner five or six dike prisms lie together. Two rectangular slab uprights 1.5 feet apart, 13 feet from the front edge, 3.5 feet from the east edge of the terrace are standing in a line parallel to the front wall; they show 2 feet above the ground. From the uprights a trough-like depression a foot deep runs to the front edge of the terrace. This site was occupied as a survey station by Sereno Bishop in 1885.

Site 11. Terrace and small platform. The terrace measures 7 by 35 feet, and is 5 feet high. The retaining wall is perpendicular, the surface of the terrace rough and rocky and coral is scattered over both ends and to a less extent within. An upright slab stands 3 feet from the front edge and 9 feet from the east edge, and a slab is lying flat in the middle front of the terrace, 3 feet from the edge.

The platform, which lies 35 feet northeast of the terrace on the edge of a bluff overlooking the valley, is an angular structure 5 feet long and 4 feet high on the bluff side, 8 feet long and several feet high on the east or valley side. The north side and part of the west side are level with the ground. Two dike stones lie on the west edge and pieces of coral on the rough stone pavement.

Site 12. A bluff shelter, about 20 feet long and 5 feet deep, and has been slightly terraced to form a level floor. Though high up in the bluff, it is easily accessible.

Site 13. Terrace on a very steep slope. As observed from Site 14 it appeared to be 18 feet long, 6 feet wide, and 4 feet high.

Site 14. Series of terraces (fig. 5). The three main terraces, averaging 70 feet in length, are 10 to 28 feet wide, separated by thick, low walls and bounded on the east side by a similar wall. Upon the terraces and also added to them are smaller terraces. There are no pavements or uprights, and the ground for the most part is sloping and uneven and appears to be adapted only for gardening. However, a house may have stood on the small division on the extreme west, or on the larger division on the extreme east. At the northwest corner is an enclosure 5 by 8 feet with a small opening on the west.

Site 15. Two terraces, possibly house sites, surrounded at the back and sides by scattered, low garden terraces. 1, Terrace 20 feet long, 13 feet wide, including a wall 3 feet wide and 2 feet high at the back and west end. In the middle of the west wall is an opening 1 foot wide. The front and east retaining walls are 2 feet wide making an area of level soil on the terrace 8 feet wide and 18 feet long. The back wall acts as a retaining wall for the earth bank at the rear of the terrace. 2, Terrace 12 feet long, 4 feet wide at the west end but rapidly widening to 8 feet at the east end. The west end wall is 2.5 feet high and 2 feet wide. There is no wall or terrace at the rear.

Site 16. Four garden terraces averaging 2 feet high and 3 feet wide, on a very steep part of a valley side.

Site 17. A series of 12 or 13 garden terraces, 4 feet wide and 1 to 2 feet high.

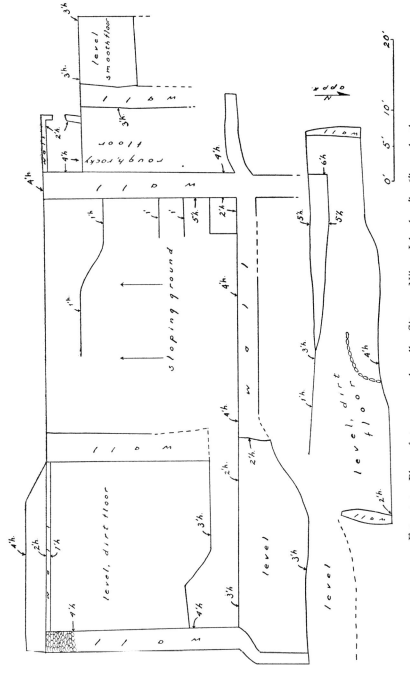

FIGURE 5.—Plan of terraces and walls, Site 14, Nihoa Island; 2'h, 6'h, and other figures on the margin indicate height of wall.

Site 18.   Terrace on the edge of a low bluff and a walled cave at its foot. The terrace is 3.5 feet high, 21 feet long, 8 feet wide on east end, and 11 feet wide on west end.   A wall 2 feet wide, and 2 to 3 feet high surrounding the rim of the terrace is broken in the middle of the west end by an entrance 3 feet wide.   The enclosing wall continues the front retaining wall to an average height of 4.5 feet.

The cave is oval in shape, 12 feet deep, 9 feet wide, and 5 feet high at the entrance.   The floor is an earth terrace faced with stone, and the retaining wall of the terrace is continued nearly to the roof of the grotto by a wall 6 feet wide at the base and 4 feet wide at the top.   The entrance to the shelter is an opening 3 feet wide in the middle of this wall.   On either side of the entrance a slab of stone has been set upright on the top of the wall and leaning against the outer edge of the roof of the cave, thus forming on both sides of the doorway a window about a foot square.   Sifting the 2 feet of soil on the floor of this shelter uncovered about 25 waterworn vesicular stones twice the size of an egg, a quantity of charcoal, and fragments (B. 7478 and B. 7479) of two stone bowls.   The bowl fragments were at the back of the cave about 8 inches below the surface, the charcoal and pebbles about the middle front of the cave 5 inches below the surface.

Site 19.   Cave shelter and garden terraces (Pl. II, *B*).   The natural cave is 12 feet long at the mouth, and 7 feet deep, but the floor has been extended 5 feet by a stone-faced earth terrace 10 feet high and with a slope greater than is usual for Nihoa walls.   A short sheltering wall has been added to each side of the cave.   On the front of the terrace, half-buried in the earth, lay a jar (B 7476).   At the back of the cave and in line with the center, a pillow of compressed bunch grass over a foot square and 3 inches thick lay under 2 inches of dust over 12 inches of soil.   Directly under the pillow was a naturally polished stone, 4.3 inches long, shaped like a lima-bean (B. 7467).   Excavation revealed three large oblong stones placed on edge and forming three sides of a fireplace box, within which were ashes and small pieces of charcoal.   The fireplace was in the middle of the floor with the upper edges level with the floor.

In shallow dirt at the northwest corner of the floor was a smooth pebble .7 inch in diameter (B. 7494) and nearly half of a kukui nut shell, possibly carried there by birds.   (On top of Necker Island half of a kukui nut with some of the kernel still within it was seen.)   In the central part of the shelter floor and somewhat nearer the front were two waterworn stones averaging 8 inches long and 5 inches in diameter and lying a few inches under the surface.   At 6 inches below the surface the small adz shown in figure 19, *c* was found, and at 8 inches a piece of a compact, light red stone which seems to be a section of an adz in the rough (B. 7444).

At the base of the west bank of Middle Valley and between Site 18 and Site 19 runs a terrace 2 feet high and averaging 5 feet wide, interrupted 16 feet from the cave at Site 18 by rough ground and a transverse dividing line of large stones. Higher up on the bank is a lower and shorter terrace.

Site 20. An earth terrace 17 feet wide, 29 feet long. The southwest corner is 2 feet high, the southeast, 4 feet high. At the southeast corner are lying a number of coral heads. The front retaining wall is badly broken down.

Site 21. Terrace. A small rough terrace of rock, estimated as about 1.5 feet high, 12 feet long, and 6 feet wide. Coral fragments are scattered over it. No uprights.

Site 22. A terrace (fig. 6) 14 feet long, 9 feet wide, similar to Site 21. Pieces of coral (not the smooth pieces of a pavement) are scattered upon it.

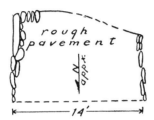

FIGURE 6.—Plan of small terrace, Site 22, Nihoa Island.

Site 23. Rock shelters. Two overhanging ledges, a camp site of the Tanager Expedition. The western shelter is 30 feet long and 6 feet deep with the floor projecting another 6 feet along the surface of a natural ledge. The eastern shelter has a wider floor shelf but less roof. That both these shelters were occupied in early times is shown by beach pebbles and a square stone fireplace in the west shelter and two short upright stones at the back of the east shelter.

Site 24. Garden terraces (Pls. IV, *A* and VI, *A*) covering several acres. A quarter of an acre of the finest and best preserved agricultural terraces on the island comprising three sites of 9 to 12 terraces was cleared. The terraces are 1.5 to 2 feet high and average 4 feet wide. Each terrace of the west set averages 18 feet long, of the middle set, 13 feet, and of the east set, 19 feet. The terraces are entirely unpaved and the soil is level with the retaining walls. Repeated and careful search resulted in finding no artifact.

Site 25. House terrace 19.5 feet long, 17 feet wide, and 2 feet high, with a back wall 4 feet high and 3 feet wide, which serves as a retaining wall for the hill slope. Each end of the terrace is enclosed by a low wall. At the northeast inner corner of the site a recess 2 feet square and 2 feet high has been left at the base of the north enclosing wall. The floor of the site is unpaved and without uprights; no artifacts lay on the surface.

Site 26. Small enclosure, similar to the stone wall shelter at Site 5. The enclosed space measures 4 by 8 feet and extends along the ridge; walls are 2 to 3 feet wide and 2 feet high. At the northwest corner is the entrance, 2 feet wide and facing up the ridge. No pavement, coral, uprights, nor artifacts were found.

Site 27. Stone wall shelter. The shelter takes up the northeast corner of a rectangular area 11 by 18 feet, the rest of which is cleared of stone and marked off on the east by a low wall, on the south by a line of stones, and on the west by a line of stones extending 5 feet from the southwest corner. The enclosure is 7 feet wide on the north and south, and 8 feet long, and includes an area 2.5 by 6 feet extending north and south, bounded by walls 2 feet high. The entrance on the south seems to be at the lowest part of the enclosing wall, and so opening onto the prepared, level area.

Site 28. A platform (fig. 7) 13.5 by 18 feet extending across a ridge, partly enclosed on the east by a wall 3 feet wide and not more than 3 feet high. The position of the seven dike prism uprights, 6 inches to 18 inches high, is shown in the plan. Sixteen feet from the northwest corner is a "stone shade"; a rounded pile of stones, 5 feet in diameter, so layed up as to form a chamber 1.5 feet in diameter, 30 inches high, and partly open to the light on the east side.

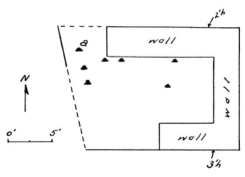

Figure 7.—Plan of Site 28, Nihoa Island: *a,* one of 7 dike prism uprights; 2'h, 3'h, height of walls.

Site 29. Terrace 13.5 by 30 feet, 2 feet high at the southwest corner, 5.5 feet high at the southeast corner. The front retaining wall is carefully built and the whole structure has the appearance of a house foundation, although no household objects were found on or about it. A low and rough wall runs from the southwest corner of the terrace to the top of a ridge.

Site 30. Several acres of small, scattered, garden terraces including two terraces near Site 31, which are about 30 feet long and only 3 feet wide.

Site 31. Series of two terraces. The first one is 16 feet wide, and 24 feet long at the front retaining wall which is 3 feet high, and 21 feet long at the back which adjoins the second terrace. Probably a house site, though no utensils or implements were found on the surface. The second terrace is 3 feet high and extends back 22 feet narrowing to 14 feet. The retaining wall exhibits fine workmanship with large stones. The rear boundaries are not very clear. The ground though fairly horizontal is irregular, probably a garden spot.

Site 32. Cave shelter. Terraced and partly walled, 20 feet long, 7 feet deep, and 3 feet high at the west end, 4 feet deep and 2 feet high at the east end. Except for two window openings the east end is closed by a wall 16 feet long which bends outward from the roof of the cave, beginning at a point 7 feet from the eastern end.

Site 33. Terraced 16 by 22 feet, and 2.5 feet high. The front retaining wall is uneven, and broken down owing to loose construction, the uneven floor indicates that the terrace was used for gardening.

Site 34. Terraces (fig. 8). A terrace 30 feet long, 8 feet wide on the west, 12 feet wide on the east. A small terrace 8.5 feet long and 6 feet wide joins the northern half of the east end at right angles. The front retaining wall of the large terrace bulges out several feet on the east end and from a height of .5 feet at the southwest corner rises to 4.5 feet towards the east.

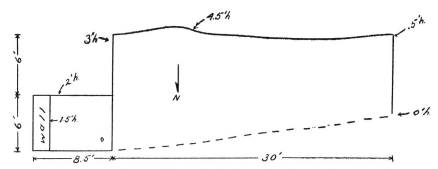

FIGURE 8.—Plan of Site 34, Nihoa Island: o'h, 4.5'h and other figures on the margin, height of walls.

The floor of the small terrace is several inches higher than that of the large terrace and a loose wall of small stones, 2 feet high and 2.5 feet wide, extends along its east edge. Lying at the northwest corner of the small terrace was the broken end of a large oblong waterworn stone (B. 7473). Of the two terraces, the smaller appears likely to have been a dwelling site.

Site 35. A terrace 26 feet long, 8 feet wide, and 2 feet high, loosely constructed.

Site 36. An exceedingly well built terrace 6 by 33.5 feet and 4.5 feet high. Up slope from this structure are numerous small garden terraces none of them having as great width, length, or height, or showing anywhere near such careful workmanship. A trench 2 feet deep was excavated 2 feet back of the front retaining wall and half the length of the terrace and another trench at right angles was cut through to the front wall, but this work revealed no artifacts. The floor, excavated, consisted of dirt and small stones. The retaining walls of the terrace consist of large somewhat rectangular stones, laid with their ends to the front at the corners of the front wall, and elsewhere with an end or a side in the face of the wall. (See Pl. V, *B*.) The front wall appears perpendicular but in reality slopes backward from the base. The side walls are perpendicular. The top courses and the lower courses of the walls are alike laid with as large rocks; the interstices are partly filled with small, irregular stones.

Site 37. A small terrace 6 by 9 feet and 2 feet high. The back wall, 3 feet high, serves as a retaining wall for the valley slope behind the terrace; the side walls rise gradually from the front to the back. Though lying in a dry stream bed, it had not been disturbed by freshets.

Site 38. An area of 3 to 4 acres of hill slope dotted with small garden terraces, some of them mere pockets of earth braced by a few stones, others as long as 20 feet and as wide as 12 feet, but all of them showing loose wall construction. This area of terracing extends as a belt about 200 feet wide from just back of Site 36 to 50 feet east of Site 37, then eastward to a point 100 feet west of Site 51. At the lower border lies the largest terrace, Site 39.

Site 39. Terraces. A terrace 13 by 24 feet and 4 feet high, lying across a dry stream bed, and smaller terrace 6 feet to the east and therefore higher on the slope. The smaller terrace is 9 by 13 feet and 4 feet high, supported on the ground slope at the back by a retaining wall 3 feet high. The floor of the larger terrace is uneven, whereas that of the smaller is level, and therefore the more likely site for a house. No uprights or artifacts were found on either.

Site 40. Terraces (fig. 9). A terrace 22.5 feet long, 10.5 feet wide, and 6 feet high, joined at each end by a projecting terrace. The west flanking terrace measures 7 feet along the front, 13 feet deep; separated from the main terrace by a wall. The top of the flanking terrace is 2 feet below the level of the center terrace and projects 4 feet beyond its front wall. The eastern terrace, which projects 10 feet, is 16 feet wide along the back, which is level with the front wall of the center terrace.

The central terrace has 13 standing dike prism uprights (Pl. IV, *B*; fig. 9) arranged from east to west in three rows of 3 ranks, and 3 uprights stand outside and to the west of the ranks. The front and middle row of uprights are in nearly perfect alignment, the rear row curves backward a foot. The dike prisms are buried in the terrace to a depth of from 1 to 2 feet and

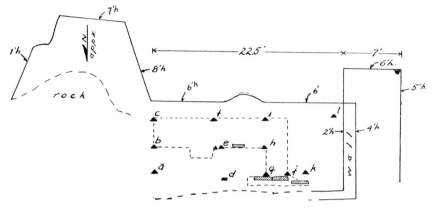

FIGURE 9.—Plan of three terraces, Site 40, Nihoa Island: *a-l*, dike prisms standing upright. The area enclosed by dotted lines was excavated down to the original ground level.

the unbroken ones stand up above the surface 1.5 to 2.5 feet. Several prisms lying on the front retaining wall and at its base may have stood on the terrace with the others, but the uprights found were firmly in place. An L-shaped trench (fig. 9) 2 to 3 feet deep and sunk presumably to ground level, revealed no objects of significance except 4 natural stone slabs placed on edge. Three of these slabs, averaging 3 by 6 by 24 inches, lay one foot beneath the surface next to uprights (fig. 9, *g* and *j*); such a slab was found between uprights *h* and *e*. I suggest that this fourth slab was part of a hearth such as was found at Site 41, and that the other slabs lay along the margin of a house. On the slopes below the terraces part of a broken bowl (B. 7486) and a piece of coral (*Pocillopora*) were collected.

Site 41. Terrace (fig. 10 and Pl. VII, *A*), joining Site 40 on the east, 28 feet long, 18 feet wide and 8 feet high, enclosed at the back by a low bluff and at each end by a sloping wall. Twelve dike splinters arranged mainly in three rows are standing upright on the terrace. The middle row has the tallest uprights, which stand 3 feet above the ground. One upright slanting outward is planted in the top of the front retaining wall. The bases of all standing uprights are at least a foot beneath the surface of the terrace. Several dike splinters lie partly exposed on the surface (fig. 10, *e*). While digging, some six other prostrate dike splinters came to light. Unfortunately their number and position were not recorded. Towards the rear of the terrace are the exposed top edges of three stone slabs set on edge and forming three sides of a fire box, which contained some charcoal.

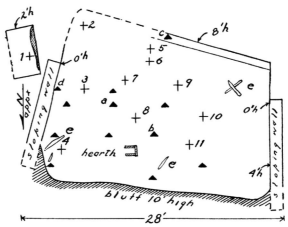

FIGURE 10.—Plan of Site 41, Nihoa Island: *a-d,* position of 4 of 12 standing dike prisms; *e,* position of fallen dike splinters; 1, position of bowl fragment (B. 7483); 2, grindstone (B. 7453); 3, maul (fig. 18); 4, conical grooved stone (Pl. XIX, *G*); 5, bowl (Pl. XVIII, *B*); 6, adz reject (fig. 20, *d*); 7, sand-stone sinker (fig. 67, *a*); 8, complete, finished adz (fig. 19, *b*); 9, Hawaiian cup-mortar (Pl. XV, *F*); 10, complete bowl (Pl. XVII, *D*); 11, grindstone (B. 7451); position unrecorded, bowl fragment (B, 7488), beach-worn coral slab (B. 7848), a chipped hammerstone (B. 7449), and two coarse grained waterworn stones.

Adjoining the terrace on the east is a diverging terrace, 6 feet long and 3 feet wide, bounded on its west side by a prostrate dike splinter 5 feet long. On the middle of this terrace and several inches under the surface was found part of the bottom of a bowl (B. 7483). Excavation of the entire structure revealed nothing more.

On the main terrace were unearthed, besides a score of waterworn stones: 5 bowls, 3 adzes, 2 grindstones, 2 sinkers, a coral slab, a hammerstone, and 2 pebble implements. Only the area enclosed by uprights *a, b,* and *c,* was thoroughly excavated and sifted. At no place was the digging carried deeper than 2 feet—the depth to undisturbed strata. Artifacts were found to a depth of 1 foot at upright *b,* but most of the objects lay 2 to 4 inches under the surface. The Hawaiian cup mortar (Pl. XV, *F*) was buried 8 inches, the bowl (Pl. XVIII, *B*) about 6 inches, the small finished adz (fig. 19, *b*), 8 inches.

On the front slope of the main terrace were twelve other artifacts: **5** bowls or bowl fragments (Pls. XVIII, *A, E*; B. 7484, B. 7485); 1 adz (fig. 19, *a*) and two rejects (fig. 20, *a, b*); 2 grindstones (B. 7452, B. 7461); and two waterworn stone implements (B. 7465, B. 7447).

Site 42. Terraces (fig. 11), 22 feet long, 15 feet wide, 8 feet high, joined on the east by a terrace 19 feet long, 12 to 16 feet wide, 8 feet high. The front wall of the east terrace sets back 4.5 feet from the front wall of the larger terrace and its floor rises a foot higher. The floors of the two terraces are not separated either by a stone wall nor by a line of stones.

On the larger terrace are two standing dike splinters, one at the middle front leaning inward and one at the back (fig. 11). Both of them stand about 2 feet above the ground. I recorded no fallen uprights on the terrace, but at its foot lay several dike splinters. Two flat, oblong waterworn stones (B. 7466 and B. 7472), 5 to 6 inches long, were found lying on the surface of the larger terrace. No excavation was made at this site.

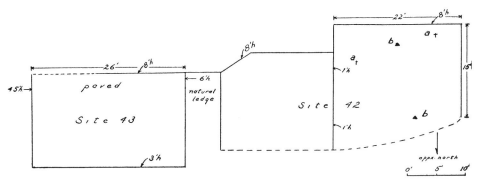

FIGURE 11.—Plan of Sites 42 and 43, Nihoa Island: *a,* location of smooth, flat, oblong beach stones; *b,* standing dike prisms; 8'h, 3'h, and other figures on margin indicate height of walls.

Site 43. Terrace (fig. 11 and Pl. V, *A*), 26 feet long, 16 feet wide, and 8 feet high, joined by a ledge with Site 42, above which it rises 6 feet. The almost vertical retaining walls are typical for East Palm Valley and other places on Nihoa.

Along the rear of the terrace a wall 3 feet high acts as a retaining wall to the sloping ground at the back. About 10 feet behind the terrace is a garden terrace 10 feet long, 3 feet wide, 2 feet high. Lying at the foot of the front retaining wall of the terrace were three or four dike prisms. Though no utensils were found on the large terrace, the pavement of small rough stones on the front quarter of its perfectly level floor strongly suggests a house site.

Site 44. Terraces (fig. 12). A series of three main terraces averaging 35 feet long, 20 feet wide, and 4.5 feet high, located near the head of the valley, in the valley bottom, and shaded by a large grove of fan palms. Each

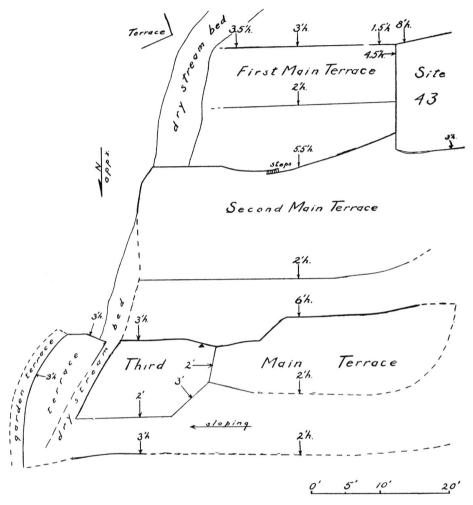

FIGURE 12.—Plan of Site 44, Nihoa Island: 3.5′h, 3′h, and other figures on the margin, height of wall.

main terrace has a low terrace, 2 feet high, at the back. The second main terrace has an unusual approach, a diagonal rough stairway of stone steps set in its front wall. Only one upright was recorded (fig. 12). Others may be hidden by the palm trees and underbrush which was not cleared away. A search over the surface of the terraces brought no archaeological finds.

Across the dry stream bed at the east margin of the large terraces are two small terraces.

Site 45. A low, almost completely natural earth terrace (fig. 13), 17 feet long and 13 feet wide, in which are standing 5 upright splinters of dike rock. Near upright *b* (fig. 13) a dike splinter about 8 inches long was almost completely buried. It may have been broken from one of the other uprights, but I did not try to match it with them. Time was insufficient for excavating this site. The depth to which the columns were buried was ascertained by extracting them.

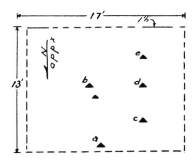

FIGURE 13.—Plan of Site 45, Nihoa Island: *a-e,* dike prisms standing upright (*a,* 2'9" long, 1'3" buried; *b,* 4'4" long, 1'2" buried; *c,* 2'7" long, 1'6" buried; *d,* 4' long, 1'7" buried; *e,* 4' long, 1'3" buried).

Site 46. Terrace and wall. A small, rude terrace about 10 feet long, 6 feet wide, 3 feet high, and having an uneven surface. Its front retaining wall utilizes several boulders in a natural position. The detached wall is simply a line of stones about 15 feet long, 2 courses high, extending along the west edge of a dry stream bed. It is much in ruins and may have been a small garden patch destroyed by freshets.

Site 47. Terrace and cave. A terrace 18 feet in length, 7.5 feet in width, and 5 feet in height. A retaining wall 2 feet high extends along the back. The surface of the south end is uneven.

Site 48. Terraces. A terrace 54 feet long, 10 feet wide on the south end, 28 feet wide on the north end, 5.5 feet high at the northwest corner. Its height at the middle of the front wall is 3.5 feet but the whole terrace rises from this point by an irregular step to a level at the south end which is about 2 feet higher than the north end. A low wall extends along the front of the south end.

The terrace rests against the base of a bluff. At the back of the south end of the terrace rises a ledge about 5 feet high upon which rests a terrace 11 feet long, 6.5 feet wide, in front of a cave 4.5 feet wide, 4 feet high at the mouth, and 6 feet deep. A little water drips from the roof of the cave, and resting on its floor were several dike splinters. In front of the cave on the small terrace, lay a grindstone (B. 7454) and, half-buried, the incomplete bowl shown in Plate XVIII, *D*. Adjoining this small terrace on the north and several feet lower, is an irregular terrace 17 feet long, with a retaining wall 3.5 feet high. On the edge of the low bluff back of these terraces is a terrace 14 feet long, 6 feet wide, 5 feet high.

On the large, lowest terrace are two dike uprights: one at the northwest corner 4 feet from the front retaining wall, and 1 foot from the north end retaining wall; the other 8 feet from the front and 18 feet from the north end. The central upright is a slab about 6 inches wide and rising 1 foot above the ground. No implements or utensils were found on the terrace or on the slope below it, which was cleared of brush.

Site 49. Terraces. Two terraces joining end on, and a third terrace up hill from them. The first terrace which is 20 feet long, 8 feet wide, and 3 feet high begins a few feet northwest from the large, lower terrace of Site 48. Its front retaining wall is loosely constructed; the southern end is somewhat broken down. Ajoining this terrace on the north, and 2 feet lower, is another rough terrace, 40 feet long and averaging 12 feet wide and 4.5 feet high. The front retaining wall turns almost at a right angle 14 feet from the south end, and after 4 feet turns again and follows a line roughly parallel to the rear boundary wall. The north end has no retaining wall, the terrace disappearing in the natural valley slope. Behind and above this terrace is a terrace 11 feet long, 10 feet wide, and 3 to 4 feet high. Its rear boundary walls are poorly defined; the south end wall makes a right angle turn 3 feet from the front and extends the length of the terrace, 2 feet.

Site 50. Terraces with upright slabs (fig. 14 and Pl. VI, *B*). A series of five terraces which have had more than the ordinary care bestowed upon their construction and which, from the conventional arrangement of the dike stone uprights upon them appear to have served a religious rather than a utilitarian purpose. Their surfaces are level and unpaved. Though fragments of coral were found on the lowest terrace, a careful search and excavations in the lowest terraces and the highest terraces revealed no other archaeological objects. Curiously an upright dike splinter stands at the base of the nearly perpendicular front wall. With the exception of a short dike splinter (fig. 14), which may have been intended for an upright, the uprights are flat or square slabs firmly planted and rising 6 to 18 inches above the ground. (For the arrangement of uprights see fig. 14 and pp. 14-15.)

The second terrace is 10 feet wide and rises only 1.5 feet above the lowest terrace. It has a single upright, which is at the back center against the front wall of the third terrace. The front wall of the second terrace is not equal in length to that of the first or the fourth terraces; but the rear lengths of the second and third terraces correspond with the length of the first. This unusual feature is clearly shown in figure 14. The fifth or top terrace is simply a levelled area 5 feet wide, and 2 feet above the fourth.

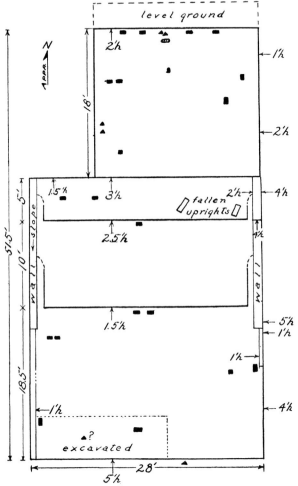

FIGURE 14.—Plan of two maraes, Site 50, Nihoa Island: rectangles, dike slab uprights; triangles, dike prism uprights; dotted line on the lowest terrace outlines the area excavated to a depth of 2 feet; 4'h and other figures on the margin, indicate height of walls.

Site 51. A great, solitary platform (fig. 15), 48 feet long, 23 feet wide, 9 feet high at the head of East Palm Valley. At its west end are arranged a number of dike splinter uprights. At the center of the terrace are two broad upright slabs, each projecting 20 inches above the ground and buried a foot in the ground. At the southeast corner of the structure is a rectangular area 10 feet long and 12 feet deep paved with large, rough, and loosely placed stones. Over it are scattered coral heads, and on a rectangular cairn at the northeast corner a few coral heads have been placed. At the west base and at the north of the cairn an upright slab projects 8 inches above the ground.

Site 52. Three or four fair sized garden terraces.

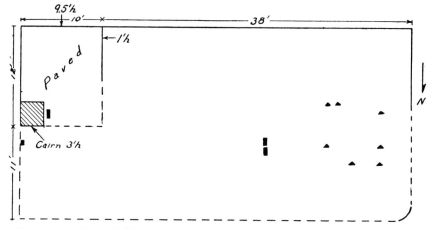

FIGURE 15.—Plan of Site 51, Nihoa: rectangles, dike slab uprights; triangles, dike prism uprights; 9.5′h, 1′h, 3′h, height of walls.

Site 53. A massive, half-natural terrace 16 feet long and 7 feet wide on the ridge between East Palm Valley and East Valley. Its retaining wall reaches a maximum height of 6 feet. The terrace supports an enclosure 10 feet square bounded by walls not more than 2 feet high. In the up-slope wall of the enclosure is a gap 2 feet wide.

Site 54. Twenty yards below Site 53 is a terrace 14 by 9 feet. Being built on an outcrop of dike rock, it is largely natural.

Site 55. A little over an acre of gentle slope dotted with small, neat garden terraces, none of which is more than 3 feet wide.

Site 56. A terrace (Pl. III, *B*), probably a house site, perched on the very edge of a bluff. Its width is about 10 feet and the height of the front retaining wall, 8 feet. It was originally about 12 feet long, but the southeast corner has tumbled into the ravine. Several waterworn stones lie on the terrace.

Site 57. Shelters (fig. 16 and Pl. III, *B*). At the rear of Site 56, a low, overhanging bluff serves as the roof for several shelters. The first shelter, the easternmost, has a terraced floor space about 15 feet long and 8 feet wide. The entrance to the cave is 6 feet high but the roof curves down rapidly towards the back. A sheltering wall, four courses of stones high and two wide, stands at the south end. While its top does not reach the roof of the cave, contact with the roof is made at the corner of the wall by means of two flat stone slabs standing on end.

The cave floor is buttressed by two terraces, the first a foot lower and 5 feet wide, upon which was a large grindstone (B. 7456) and a jar (B. 7475) half-buried, lying on its side. The outer terrace, 6 feet lower than the first, is 5 feet wide, 2 feet high. It was probably a garden patch. Upon the floor of the cave lay a broken grindstone (B. 7458), and a flat pebble showing use as a hammerstone (B. 7446 a). A foot below the floor were found ashes and bits of charcoal at the front center and at the south end a piece of gourd (B. 7400 a) and a pillow, made of several handfuls of bunch grass.

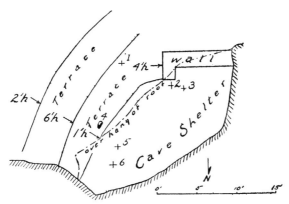

FIGURE 16.—Plan of Site 57, Nihoa Island: 2′h and other figures on the margin, height of walls: 1, large grindstone (B. 7456) on surface; 2, piece of grindstone (B. 7458) on surface where soil only 1 inch deep; 3, flat waterworn pebble (B. 7446a) partly buried; 4, complete stone jar (B. 7475) half buried; 5, piece of gourd (B. 7400a) buried several inches; 6, pillow or bed of bunch grass, buried several inches.

Site 58. Bluff shelters (fig. 17 and Pl. III, *B*). A terrace 14 feet long and 6 wide, well under the projecting ledges of a bluff and buttressed by a terrace 4 feet lower, and 3 to 6 feet wide supported by a retaining wall 10 feet high.

Upon the surface of the two terraces or buried to a depth of not more than 18 inches were found: a stone bowl fragment, 6 grindstones, 32 cowrie shells, 4 waterworn stone implements, 3 awls or needles of bird bone, a bone from which pieces had been cut, 2 thin fragments of tortoise shell, fragments of a gourd, a piece of the rim of a wooden bowl, a wooden netting shuttle, a bed of matted bunch grass, and a fishhook of human bone. Position of these objects and the catalog numbers are shown in figure 17.

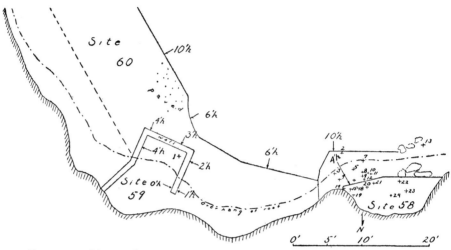

FIGURE 17.—Plan of Sites 58, 59, and 60, Nihoa Island: 10'h, 6'h, and other figures, height of walls; 1, fragment of stone bowl (B. 7487b) on surface (part of the bowl found at 7); 2, large bored cowrie (B. 7495b) on top of wall; 3, bored cowrie buried 4 inches; 4, half of waterworn pebble (B. 7448), 2 inches thick, 3.5 inches in diameter, buried; 5, piece of rim of wooden bowl (Pl. XVI, *A*) buried 4 inches; 6, grindstone (B. 7455) on surface; 7, fragment of stone bowl (B. 7487a) (part of bowl found at 1); 8, bored cowrie (B. 7495d) buried 4 inches; 9, piece of grindstone (B. 7462), buried; 10, adz in rough (?) (B. 7439), buried about 6 inches; 11, wooden netting shuttle (Pl. XVI, *B*); 12, waterworn stone (B. 7471) on surface; 13, large grindstone (B. 7457), on surface; 14, cache of 25 bored cowrie shells (B. 7495, 7495a) on surface and buried; 15, human canine tooth (B. 7847) buried several inches; 16, small rectangular piece of tortoise shell (B. 7496a); 17, splinter of human bone (Pl. XV, *B*), buried; 18, 4 bone needles (Pl. XV, *D*), buried about 8 inches; 19, 4 cowries (one taken, B. 7495f), buried; 20, grindstone too large to carry away, on surface; 21, grindstone (B. 7459); 22, grindstone in two pieces (B. 7460), on surface; 23, fishhook of human bone (Pl. XV, *C*), buried 5 inches; 24, pillow or bed of matted bunch grass. In addition to these artifacts, pieces of gourd (B. 7500b) were found near spot 16, and a flat waterworn stone (B. 7446b). A small fragment of tortoise shell (B. 7496b) was found on the upper terrace, and on the lower terrace, a pebble highly polished by use.

While excavating, ashes or bits of charcoal were found at several places on both terraces and the sieve revealed a few *opihi* shells (*Helcioniscus*).

Site 59. Enclosure (fig. 17 and Pl. III, *B*). A rectangular walled enclosure on the wide terraced ledge of a bluff and half under a projecting ledge. It is roughly 8 feet square and open on the inner side. The smaller of two fragments of a bowl (B. 7487) lay on the surface at one corner of the enclosure. The other fragment was 30 feet away on Site 58. Excavation in the shallow soil within the enclosure brought to light no other artifacts.

Site 60. A large terrace (fig. 17 and Pl. III, *B*) projecting out from a bluff and standing in the open adjoining Site 59 on the east. It is 27 feet long, 22 feet wide, and 10 feet high, and continues in a narrower terrace for 10 feet to the southeast. The front part of the platform is loosely paved with small, rough stones. Most of the front retaining wall is not only vertical but even overhangs at the southwest corner.

Site 61. Shelter. Ten feet up on the bluff above Site 60 a horizontal recess has been modified for shelter. The floor is formed by a terrace 15 feet long, with a front retaining wall 2 feet high. The floor extends back into the cave forming a habitable place with a maximum width of 12 feet. The entrance to the cave is 4 feet high, but the roof rapidly slopes towards the back. Several dike splinters lay on the front retaining wall. No objects were found on the surface or by digging in the floor of the cave. Along the bluff a few yards south of the shelter is a small niche with floor, about 2 feet square, artificially levelled by a terrace 6 inches high. On top of the bluff above the cave are several small garden terraces.

Site 62. A small bluff shelter, the floor rudely terraced. On a small natural stone shelf at the back of the cave lay the upper part of a large stone adz (fig. 20, *c*).

Site 63. Terrace. On the flattened tip of the southeastern point of the island is a very low terrace 36 feet wide along the south side, 30 feet wide along the west side, and only 12 feet wide along the east side. The eastern end slopes upward and has a rougher surface. At the northwest corner lay a large upright which had toppled over close to a large head of coral, and I remember one or two low and thick uprights at the east end.

Site 64. Bluff shelters. Two terraces, joining end on, under the overhanging thick ledge of a low bluff. The wider, easternmost terrace is only half protected by the natural roof. Some digging and sifting of the soil of this terrace resulted in no finds.

Site 65. Burial site. By following a ledge along the face of a sea cliff, Anderson and Dranga discovered bones lying in a pile at the back of the ledge where they were protected by an overhanging ledge. The disposition of the burial was the same as at Site 2. All the bones were removed and upon inspection found to represent one adult male and two children, one several years younger than the other. The bones of the adult were: the pelvic girdle, the right and left tarsals nearly complete, several metatarsals, the left fibia, the right ulnar, the right scapula, and 10 vertebra. The infant bones were: one occipital, a left parital, part of left maxillary, part of lower right jaw, 2 pair femora, pair of inominatum, and one os inominatum.

Site 66. Bluff shelter. Cooke discovered a bluff cave shelter 400 feet north of Site 65. Upon the floor of the terrace in front of the cave lay three complete stone jars (figs. 22, *a, b*; Pl. XVII, *B*) partly buried and a piece of breadfruit wood (Pl. XVI, *C*) which had been shaped into a crude tiller of European form.

ARCHAEOLOGICAL SPECIMENS

STONE IMPLEMENTS

HAMMERSTONES

The natives living on Nihoa must have had stones used as hammers if only to shape the adzes and bowls. Of the stone artifacts found by the Tanager Expedition several are well adapted to hammering, but one only, B. 7449, from Site 41, is clearly specialized for this purpose. It is an oblong, partially worked stone, 8.5 inches long, rectangular in cross section, 2.5 inches wide, 1.9 inches thick. Both ends are rounded by battering and pounding. Its shape suggests that the chipping upon it was done with the intention of shaping it into an adz. It weighs 2½ pounds.

Flat, oval, waterworn stones, 3 to 6 inches long and weighing 10 ounces to 2.5 pounds, show battered ends from use as hammers.

FIGURE 18.—Maul from Site 42, Nihoa Island: Length 7 inches, width 2.5 inches, thickness 2.8 inches, weight 3.5 pounds; top and sides ground smooth, back roughly chipped.

Like the middle section of a very large adz is the implement, probably a maul (fig. 18), found at Site 42. Both extremities are bounded by a natural surface, proving that the implement was not originally longer.

GRINDSTONES

Thirteen grindstones were transported from Nihoa, several were left because of their weight, although one weighing 57 pounds, probably the largest, was brought to Honolulu. The grindstones are slabs or prisms from the numerous dikes, worn smoothly and often deeply on one or two faces. They were found on or near the dwelling sites.

One entire face is worn to its very edges and shows a shallow concavity but no sharp grooves. The scratches on the coarser grained grindstones show unmistakably that the motion of grinding was in straight lines and most of it lengthwise of the stone. The smooth hollow indicates that the greatest pressure was exerted on approaching the center of the grindstone and that the object being ground was more frequently passed over this part.

The grindstones gathered at any one place do not constitute a series of grinding surfaces from very coarse to very fine, but some have a little smoother surface than the others, and of most stones ground on two surfaces, one surface is more worn than the other. The ten grindstones at the lower bluff shelters in East Valley were surely not intended for ten different stages in the shaping and finishing of an object, but for convenience: several men might wish to be working at the same time or might wish to use a particular stone. It is probable that the last of the natives who lived or camped at this site brought there ready made grindstones which they found at deserted sites.

Three large grindstones were found in the upper part of East Palm Valley at Site 41, and one at Site 48. The dwellers at the other sites surely had grindstones which would have been found had they not been removed. No stones bearing marks of grinding were found in place.

The grindstones may be grouped into two classes: 1, large, flat stones ground on both sides and perhaps serving also for platters; 2, heavy blocks of stone having a smaller grinding surface, four of the six specimens worn on only one side.

The heaviest, flat grindstone (B. 7450 from Site 57) is triangular in outline, 12 inches wide, 14 inches long, worn deeply, and completely to the edges on both faces. It weighs 57 pounds.

But the flat grindstone having the largest grinding surface, from Site 41, weighs only 17 pounds. It measures 11 by 15.5 inches and is .5 to 2.5 inches thick. One face is worn deeply concave, the other has a wide groove worn.

The other flat grindstones—all ground on both sides except B. 7456— are: B. 7452 from Site 41, 10 inches wide, 16 inches long, 37.5 pounds; B. 7453 from Site 41, 10 by 10 inches, .75 inches thick; B. 7454 from Site 48, 10 by 12 inches, 1.5 inches thick; B. 7455 from Site 58, 5 by 12 inches, 1.5 inches thick; B. 7456 from Site 41, 7 by 8 inches, 2 inches thick.

The six block or prism grindstones are: B. 7457 from Site 58, length 16 inches, width of one grinding face, 5.5 inches, width of the adjoining face also used for grinding but not so deeply worn, 3.5 inches, and weight, 28 pounds (this piece is also worn on the back); B. 7458 from Site 57, broken section of a grindstone worn on both faces, weight 11.5 pounds; B. 7459 from Site 58, 9 inches long, 7 inches wide, 3.5 inches thick; B. 7460 from Site 58, 8 inches long, 6 inches wide, 3 inches thick, and in two pieces which had long been separated; B. 7461 from Site 41, 9.5 inches long, 4 inches wide, a dike prism or splinter; B. 7462 from Site 58, 7 inches long, 3.5 inches wide, 6 pounds in weight, a fragment of a larger stone.

The score of deeply worn grindstones lying upon or buried in the house platforms or floors of bluff shelters proves that the adzes in the Bishop Museum are a very small part of those once in use on Nihoa. The diligent search made by the Tanager Expedition certainly would have revealed a larger number, unless, as is probable, they were hidden by the natives, or taken with them upon leaving the island. Raiders or casual visitors could not have gathered up most of the adzes once used on Nihoa; they may, however, have brought adzes to grind, thus partly accounting for the excess of grindstones. If visitors are responsible for the wear on the grindstones, their visits must have been long or frequent.

CORAL RUBBING STONE

A rubbing stone of coral, having a rectangular base 3.25 by 3.75 inches, and one inch thick, and a knob handle 1.3 inches high (Pl. XV, *A*), was collected on Nihoa in 1885. Evidently a pierced lug for a suspension cord originally existed on one end, as what appears to be its stumps are to be seen. The other end and sides as well as the bottom and top are ground flat. All surfaces meet sharply at right angles. The knob handle, which is off center, is 1.5 inches long and 1 inch wide. The top is rounded and to a less extent the corners of the sides.

ADZES

The terminology used in this paper for describing adzes is that decided upon by Buck, Emory, Skinner, and Stokes (7a).

The material of the adzes (fig. 19, *a-c*) is compact basalt of varying shades. The largest finished adz is slate-gray, the next in size, dark gray, and the smallest, olive-gray. Three rejects are blue-gray, and the fourth, olive-gray. The shaping has been done by chipping and, in the finished adzes, also by grinding. Two of the three adzes are entirely ground smooth, the third is ground smooth on the sides but only partially ground on front and back. The cross section is a rectangle with straight or very slightly convex sides. The sides of the largest and smallest adz are straight and converge towards the poll, but the sides of the medium adz are curved outward, the middle being wider than the cutting edge or the poll. The backs of the adzes are convex transversely. The tang was formed in the largest specimen by chipping on the front, and in the other two by the grinding down of the front towards the poll so that the front of the tang slopes away from the front of the blade at an angle of about 18 degrees. The chin is visible in the smallest adz and just visible on the next in size. The cutting edge is straight, viewed from above, in the largest and smallest adz, but convex in the other. Viewed from in front, it is straight in all. The poll is convex or flat.

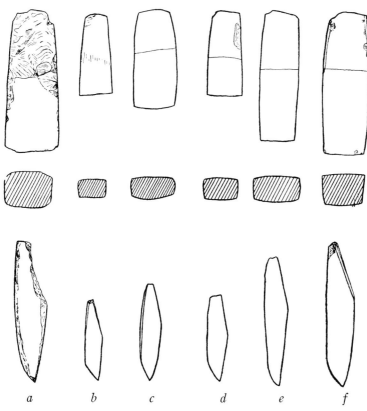

FIGURE 19.—Front, cross section at angle of tang and blade, and profile of adzes: *a, b,* from Site 41, Nihoa Island; *c,* from Site 19, Nihoa Island; *d,* from the island of Hawaii; *e,* from Kauai (No. 6323); *f,* from Waimea, Oahu (B. 2116).
(Approximately ½ natural size.)

TABLE 1. WEIGHT AND MEASUREMENTS OF ADZES AND REJECTS FROM NIHOA. (Measurements in Inches)

SPECIMEN	WEIGHT OUNCES	MAXIMUM LENGTH	MAXIMUM THICKNESS	WIDTH CUTTING EDGE	L-C INDEX[a]	L-T INDEX[b]	ILLUS- TRATION
Adz B. 7436	4	3.4	8.5	1.3	38.3	24.3	fig. 19, *a*
Adz B. 7438	1	1.95	.4	.85	44.9	20.4	fig. 19, *b*
Adz B. 7437	1.75	2.35	.47	.95	38.9	20.3	fig. 19, *c*
Reject B. 7442	11	4	1.3	1.95			fig. 20, *b*
Reject B. 7445	5	3.4	8.5	1.8			fig. 20, *a*
Reject B. 7441	30	5.7	2.3				fig. 20, *c*
Reject B. 7443	33.5	5.6	2.2				fig. 20, *d*

[a] LC index is the width of the cutting edge divided by the length of the adz, giving approximately, the proportion of breadth to length.
[b] L-T index is the maximum thickness divided by the length, giving the relative thickness.

The process of blocking and first chipping of an adz is shown by the reject, figure 20, *b*. An adz on which a faulty blow with the hammerstone took off too great a chip towards the butt is shown in figure 20, *a*. These two rejects are quadrangular in cross section, the sides sloping in towards the back. No finished adz has other than a rectangular cross section. The sides of the reject shown in figure 20, *c* converge slightly towards the poll and are ground perfectly flat. The front and back remain roughly chipped. The reject shown in figure 20, *d* is unusual in having a rectangular cross section.

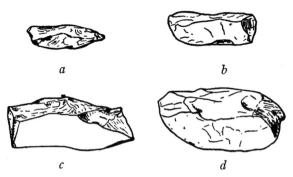

a   *b*

c   *d*

FIGURE 20.—Adz rejects from Nihoa Island: *a*, showing blocking out and first chipping; *b*, from Site 41, chipping process carried further; *c*, from Site 62, rearward part of a heavy narrow tanged adz; *d*, from Site 41, partly blocked out adz showing original surface of dike rock on its faces.
(Approximately ¼ natural size.)

KNIVES AND AWLS

The roofs of most of the bluff shelters on Nihoa are ledges of dike rock from which sharp-edged flakes are continually splitting off through weathering. Finding these flakes on the floor of the caves is no proof that they were used, although many of them are well fitted for knives or awls and must have furnished the supply of these. Because slabs and prisms of dike rock were carried onto the house sites where natural flanking continued, the finding of sharp edged or pointed bits of dike rock here, also, is no indication that any particular specimen is an implement. One of these flakes (B. 7469) is 2.5 inches long, 1.2 inches wide, and weighs half an ounce. It has two sharp edges and a point.

MISCELLANEOUS ARTIFACTS

The only coral file known from Nihoa is the fine specimen shown in figure 21. By grinding, one side and one end have been brought to a sharp edge. A hole has been bored in the top for a suspension string. The specimen would serve equally well as a scraper for fish scales.

A 13-pound, conical, flat-bottomed stone, encircled by a wide groove near the top (Pl. XIX, *G*) was dug up at Site 41. (See fig. 10.) The horizontal cross section is a true oval. The shaping is natural except for the groove, a pecked depression 1 inch in diameter and ¼ inch deep near the center of the

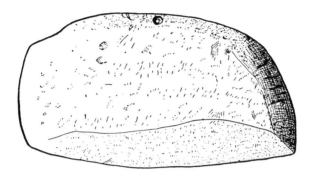

FIGURE 21.—Coral file or scraper from Nihoa: Length 5.5 inches, width 3.2 inches, thickness 1.4 inches, weight 14 ounces, hole bored at the top is 0.1 inch in diameter. (Collected by W. E. H. Deverell in 1885.)

bottom, and possibly the bottom, which seems to have been worn smooth and flat by grinding or rubbing. No stones resembling this are in the Bishop Museum. I would hazard the guess that it was being shaped into a bowl.

In the floor dust of Site 58 were four needles of slender bird bone (Pl. XV, *D*) which may be tattooing implements or needles for sewing tapa. The joint at one end is well suited for the tapping hammer; it is equally suited for holding a line in threading but would make a hole .2 inches in diameter if passed through any material. The two with unbroken points measure 3.8 and 3.4 inches long, respectively. The diameter of all averages .1 inches. The point is .5 inches long and is formed by making a long, slanting cut. A great many of the tattooing instruments from Tahiti, the Marquesas, and Samoa are preserved in museums, but nothing is known of the instruments used by the Hawaiians. It may be that the Hawaiians used a simple instrument of sharpened bird bone, which would escape especial notice. Hawaiian tapa-sewing needles are also lacking in collections.

A very much decayed wooden netting shuttle was found at Site 58 (fig. 17), 7.5 inches long (Pl. XVI, *B*). The broken two prongs of one end are preserved and also one of the other end. The longest prong is .5 inches long. The width of the shuttle in the middle is .5 inches, the thickness .2 inches. The sides are rounded.

CONTAINERS

VESSELS

Twenty-five stone vessels from Nihoa are represented by fragments or complete specimens. All are fashioned by the laborious process of excavating rounded beach stones of vesicular basalt, and more or less reducing the original surface.

Bowls.—Five bowls are sub-spherical with a maximum diameter of 7.25 to 9.25 inches and a height ranging from 5 to 7 inches. The smallest bowl and the largest complete bowl are shown in Plate XVIII, *A, B.* Their water capacity is 32 and 72 ounces. The mouth is not perfectly circular or elliptical. The excavation is to within 1.5 to 2 inches from the bottom. The sides thicken uniformly from .25 inches at the rim to the thickness of the bottom. The rim is convex; the interior surface is even though not especially smooth. The outer surface is uneven in all but the smallest bowl and is the natural surface of the beach-worn stone. The maximum diameter of the cavity attained is one-third of the distance below the rim.

Jars.—The common Nihoa vessel—common because there are 13—has a thinner shell, is proportionately taller, more extensively excavated, and much more skillfully worked. The exterior preserves closely the original shape of the beach stone but in half of the jars not any of the original surface. The rim is ground flat in the four most finished specimens (Pl. XVII, *A, B*; fig. 22, *a, b*).

a   *b*   *c*

FIGURE 22.—Longitudinal cross section of vessels: *a*, stone jar from Site 66, Nihoa Island; *b*, stone jar from Site 66, Nihoa Island showing incomplete interior excavation; *c*, Hawaiian wooden bowl (No. 11837).
(Approximately ⅛ natural size.)

The height of the jars is 5.7 to 9.3 inches, the diameter of the mouth averages 5.5 inches, the water capacity 50 ounces, the weight 7.5 pounds. Measurements, weight, and capacity of all are given in Table 2. Excavation was evidently done in steps, because in the interior of jar (fig. 22, *b*) is a rough shelf an inch below the rim, where reduction was carried to one inch from the outer surface instead of half an inch, as at the start. Excepting one (Pl. XVII, *D*), which is not deeply excavated, the greatest width of all the jars is several inches below the rim.

Pot.—A tall bowl of medium size is distinct from the others in having a flat bottom, diverging sides, and very thick sides and bottom (Pl. XVII, *E*). From its resemblance to a flower pot I have termed it a"pot." The bottom is not perfectly flat but slightly convex. The whole exterior and interior is smoothly shaped and symmetrical. The interior of the bowl, however, appears unfinished because of the extraordinary thickness of the sides when compared with all the other containers of Nihoa or Necker. Further excavation may well have been in process were the method of uniform reduction being employed, as in the Nihoa bowl (fig. *22, b*). Nihoa and Necker bowls, like the Hawaiian, were first shaped on the outside, then excavated.

The rim is rough and uneven, surely not the original rim, yet no sharp surface bespeaks a broken rim. Either excessive weathering or a rough attempt at reshaping the edges has taken place. Perhaps a break in the rim stopped the work of excavating; judging from the jars and especially from the similar Necker pot, a vessel of this diameter would have a height of 8 inches. For actual measurements see Table 2.

Elliptical bowls.—Three large bowls are elliptical in cross section and have flattened bottoms both interiorly and exteriorly. (See Pl. XVIII, *C, D*.) There is a fragment of flat bottom of another bowl evidently of this type. The exterior of the three bowls is uneven and preserves a large part of the original surface of the stone; the interior is even and smooth. The sides rise almost vertically from the bottom but curve inward towards the top. The rim is convex. Beginning an inch below the rim, the thickness of an inch continues to the bottom. Measurements are given in Table 2. Although the water capacity could not be taken with these incomplete bowls, I have computed it as being between 4 and 5 quarts.

A rectangular dish or low bowl of basalt, remarkably symmetrical and well made, was picked up at Site 41 (Pl. XVIII, *E*). The outer corners are rounded, the inner corners more sharp. The sides and bottom are convex exteriorly and concave interiorly. The sides curve abruptly inward towards the top. The thickness of the bowl throughout averages one inch.

The largest known Nihoa vessel (Table 2; Pl. XVII, *G*) was discovered by Lieut. W. H. Bainbridge, Coast and Geodetic Survey, June 1928, at the base of a bluff just below Site 19. One-fourth of the rim was projecting above the earth. It is a sharply rectangular bowl of the same pattern as the small bowl (Pl. XVIII, *E*), though less symmetrical and not so well finished. For some unexplainable reason, a jagged hole, 2/3 inches in diam-

TABLE 2.—WEIGHTS AND MEASUREMENTS OF VESSELS FROM NIHOA

| Type | Specimen | Site | Measurements in Inches | | | | | | Weight Pounds | Water Cap. Ounces | Illustration |
			Height	Maximum Diameter	At Rim	Minimum Diameter At Rim	Thickness Lips	Thickness Bottom			
bowl	B.7485	a	6.25	9.25	6.5	7	.5	1.75	13.5	72	Pl. XVIII, A
"	B.7486	41	6	9.25	?	?	.5	1.6	8.5+	?	
"	B.7487	40	7	?	?	?	.5	2	7++		
"		58	5	8	6.75	?	.5	2	5+	32	
"		41	5	7.25	6	5.5	.3	1.5	7	127	
jar		7	9.3	8.1 middle	7	6.6	.45	1.2	14	?	Pl. XVIII, B
"	B.6508	66	8.3	7.25 "	?	6.6	.4	1.1	8.75+	61	Pl. XVII, A
"	B.7475	66	7.1	6.5 "	5.9	5.5	.3	1.1	7	18	Pl. XVII, B
"	B.7476	66	6.6	4.9 "	4.4	4.1	.45	1.4	4.25	39	fig. 22, a
"	B.7481	43	8.8	6.25 near top	5	4.3	.5	1.9	9.25	51	fig. 22, b
"		57	8.25	6.3 middle	5.1	4.4	.45	.95	6	40	
"		19	7.1	6.5 "	5.5	4.45	.45	1.6	7.75	?	
"		41	7.5	5.7 "	5	?	.4	1.1	4+	51	
"		?	6.4	7.9 "	6.7	5.4	.4	.7	8.2	8.5	
"		41	5.7	5.7 near top	5	4.8	.6	3.1	6	32	Pl. XVII, C
pot		a	6	7.75	7.75	7.6	1.3	2.25	11.25	?	Pl. XVII, D
bowl		b	10.5	?	?	?	.5	1.2	11+	?	Pl. XVII, E
"	B.7482	48	10	13	?	7.5	.5	2.6	26++		Pl. XVIII, C
"		41	8	11	?	?	.5	2.1	17+		Pl. XVIII, D
"	L.2462	19	9.5	14.	11.	6.5	1.	2.	56	608	Pl. XVII, G
jar	B.7478	18	fragment of bowl—about 1/5 of lip and 4" into bowl: lip, 4" thick								
"	B.7479	18	fragment of bowl—about 1/4 of circumference at middle: 7" thick								
"	B.7480	41	fragment of bowl—about 1/5 of lip and 3" into bowl: lip and 3" thick								
bowl	B.7483	41	fragment of bowl bottom, thickness 1.25 inches								

a East Palm Valley.
b East Palm Valley, by side of platform west of middle clump of palm trees.

eter, has been pierced on each side of the bowl, near the smaller end and half way down the side.

DISHES

A dish or platter of basalt found on Nihoa in 1885 is boat-shaped, having a pointed and a flat end (Pl. XIX, *A*). It is 13.5 inches long, has a maximum width of 7.5 inches, and a height of 3.25 inches. The thickness of the bottom is 1.2 inches. The excavation was not carried fully into the tip and therefore a wide rim is left there. The exterior of the bowl is the original surface of the stone from which it was made.

GOURDS

From a bluff shelter, Site 58, several pieces of a gourd which could not have been more than 8 inches in circumference, and a piece of a much larger gourd were recovered. In the siftings at Site 57, a piece from another large gourd was found. The Hawaiian gourds belong to the species *Cucurbita maxima* and *Lagenaria vulagaris,* and the fragments of rind found on Nihoa might be either of these. These vines could have been cultivated on Nihoa as they will grow and produce fruit during the rainy season. The seeds could then be kept for the next season.

MORTAR

A basalt mortar was unearthed 8 inches below the surface at Site 41 (Pl. XV, *F*). It is identical with the small, smoothly ground, cup-shaped mortars of the Hawaiian islands, which were evidently made to hold in the hand. The material is a close-grained basalt patinated reddish-brown. There is one other specimen of this grain and color, a large grindstone; therefore, I believe the material to be local. The base is roundly conical, ground perfectly smooth. The rim is ground convex but is highest on the inside.

FISHING APPARATUS

FISHHOOKS

A fishhook of bone, probably from a human femur, was rescued from the sifting screen while excavating the floor of the bluff shelter, Site 58. (For the form see Pl. XV, *C*.) One side is convex, preserving the natural curve of the exterior surface of the bone, the other side shows part of the rough surface of the cavity of the bone. In all respects this hook is identical with certain of the Hawaiian hooks in the Bishop Museum.

A piece of bone, also probably human, was found in the same floor as the fishhook. It bears the sharp knife cuts where a small block of bone has been severed from one end (Pl. XV, *B*), undoubtedly to be shaped into a fishhook. The form suggests that it may be an awl with the point broken off. However, no grinding or wear is visible.

A cut-out block, 1.05 by .45 inches, of tortoise shell (B. 7496) came from the same dwelling floor as the last two objects. (From a fisherman's workshop on the island of Kahoolawe, several blocks of this size have been collected, though somewhat thicker, and from the same shop, tiny fishhooks made from these pieces.) A rough fragment of tortoise shell, measuring 1.5 inches across and of the same thickness as the last, was also discovered at this site, but further towards the rear of the floor. Several straight edges seem to mark where sections have been cut off.

SINKERS

A line or net sinker was excavated from Site 41. It is a flat, oval, limestone pebble having a shallow groove which encircles it longitudinally. (See fig. 67, *a.*)

That squid-lure sinkers were on Nihoa is attested by the great number of cowrie shells prepared for squid lures. But these sinkers must have been taken off the island or most carefully hidden, to entirely escape the search made by the Tanager Expedition.

SQUID-LURES

At Site 58 were found 29 cowrie shells (*Cypraea mauritiana*), all with the side opposite the lip, broken, and all bored with one or two holes for the attachment of cords to the squid hook and its sinker. Not one of these lures was found at the other sites. Would so many shells be used by the dwellers at one site and none be used by those once inhabiting the others? It is quite possible, like the grindstones which were so abundant in this immediate vicinity, that some of the shells were gathered from deserted sites. It may be that the inhabitant of this shelter may have been the only one who left his discarded lures at home, possibly with the intention of trying them out again.

The shells range from 2.8 to 4.2 inches in length, averaging 3.5 inches. The holes, which are round or elliptical, and bored from the outside, average .25 inches in length. Ten are bored with one hole in the larger end and none in the smaller. Are these unfinished, or were they used with only one hole? Such a large proportion consistently treated indicates a functional type.

The remaining 19 shells are bored at both ends, as are all the Hawaiian lures. One shell, fortunately, has a piece of braid tied to each end, thus giving a sample of Nihoa cordage and an idea of the method by which the lure was attached. (See fig. 23.)

FIGURE 23.—Cyprae shell, 3.1 inches long, with fragment of hala root fiber three-ply braid attached through holes at each end. From Site 58, Nihoa Island.

The cord is a flat, three-ply braid, .2 inches across. The fibers look like those of the coconut, but are more pliable, less strong, and have ends finely frayed. No plants now growing on Nihoa or Necker furnish fiber which might be used for cordage except the bark of *Sida cordifolia* and *Triumfetta procumbens*. Microscopic examination by Dr. Forest B. H. Brown shows that the braid on the squid lure was not made from these plants but was probably made from the aerial roots of hala or possibly of *Freycinetia*. It is reasonably certain that the Nihoa cord is not from the plants now growing on the island, or from the hau, the olona, or the coconut.

Miscellaneous Implements

What appears to be a roughly made tiller of European form is shown in Plate XVI, *C*, picked up on the floor of the bluff shelter, Site 64, by Cooke. Brown is certain that the material is breadfruit wood.

The segment of the rim of a wooden bowl some 8 inches in diameter is illustrated in Plate XVI, *A*. The section had been neatly cut off, leaving a sharp edge undoubtedly intended for scraping. A hole has been pierced approximately in the middle. The wood is too much rotted for identification.

Skeletal Material

The bones found at Site 2 were dry and brittle, the extremities of most of them disintegrated; drifting spray had permeated them with salt which crystallized out when the bones were dried after washing in the laboratory. Parts of all the skulls were missing and most of the parts of the skeletons. Petrels were nesting behind the skulls and I was then under the impression that the beating of bird's wings and the burrowing habits of the petrels would in time greatly disturb the bones and work them to the side where they would tumble over the cliff, although fallen debris would tend to protect them. Yet there seemed to be one whole skeleton missing and three pelvic girdles, and such bones as were present seemed to be very little disturbed. Around a bend to the left of the four skulls and 15 feet away, was an astragulus, a navicular, and the lower part of a fibula of a right leg covered with several inches of dust. Digging with a hand pick showed no other bones except a fragment of a frontal 20 inches nearer the edge of the cliff. Had time permitted sifting the soil along this bench a few more fragments might have been found, but the significance of the collection lies in the discovery that the frontal fragment fitted perfectly a jog in the broken frontal of the skull (no. 813) on the extreme right of the main pile of bones, also the fibia and tarsal bones seem to go with a tibia (no. 824) which lay to the right of the skulls. No natural or animal agency I can think of will explain the presence of the bones so far away from the skeletons with which they belong (rats have not been there or their teeth marks would surely have shown). It seems clear that one of the bodies lay there and subsequently the bones were gathered up and piled with the others, which would account for the skulls being all together and the long bones in a pile side by side. The missing of some bones may be accredited to the activities of the birds, of others to the apparent fact that bones were gathered up and carried from the margin of the ledge to a more protected spot.

Sifting all the dust on that part of the ledge where the main pile of bones lay revealed 4 calvaria, 1 jaw, 1 female pelvic girdle, 2 pairs tibia, 1 pair fibia, 2 pair femora, 1 left femur, pair of scapula, several vertebra, several ribs, 1 toe bone and 1 heel bone.

The bones require a careful study by an expert before their affinity with skeleton remains in Hawaii and elsewhere may be pronounced, but a few observations safely may be made here: the one fairly complete crania is decidedly dolicho-cephalic (length 192.5, breadth 138, index 71.68); the nose is broad (28) but extremely long (55), the index being 50.90; the nasal bridge is moderately high and the lower border of the nasal aperture poorly defined; the face is prognathic (alveolar projection index 108). The long bones are those of individuals not very tall, the reconstructed stature of one is approximately not over 5 feet 5 inches.

The bones found at the burial shelter, Site 65, are enumerated on page 37.

NECKER ISLAND

GEOGRAPHY

Necker Island lies 300 miles northwest of Niihau, the northernmost inhabited Hawaiian island. Its nearest neighbors, Nihoa Island and French Frigates Shoal, are far out of sight (fig. 1). The island is about one mile long and averages 400 feet wide. It comprises an area of about 41 acres. The summit ridge stands 150 to 200 feet above sea level with a culminating point at 278 feet. Necker thus has almost the length of Nihoa but is much narrower and lower, and also more barren. The island is shaped like a fish-hook, the shank extending east and west is 4,000 feet long, and the barb, the northwest cape, is 600 feet long and 200 feet wide. Its extremity is separated from the main part of the island by a gap so low that waves often splash across it. The curve of the hook encloses the shallow Shark Bay. During the blowing of the Trade Winds, the bay is too rough to allow a landing on the shelves of the north shore, but as West Cove is remarkably protected at such times, boats may come up to the narrow ledges on its south side (Pl. VIII, *B*). On the south coast inaccessible bluffs rise from the wave-cut benches (Pl. IX, *B*); but the larger part of the bluffs on the north are easily climbed (Pl. VIII, *A*), and a natural trail leads up the face of the west cliff. (See fig. 24.)

The crest of the island is flat or gently sloping to the north bluffs. The main ridge can be traversed easily from one end to the other. The slopes of Necker are partially covered with grass, pigweed, a plant resembling salt bush, and *ohai* bush, the only plants found on the island. The present vegetation of Necker is of the same type as that seen by La Perouse 150 years ago (p. 53).

Palmer (37) estimates the rainfall as 20 to 25 inches a year, and adds:

Two small seeps of ground water were found. One on the north slope of the main island [next to Bowl Cave] . . . It might be possible to collect five gallons of water a day from this seep, which appears to be due to a relatively impervious layer of lava which brings the ground water to the surface. The other seep is about thirty feet above sea level on the north side of the westernmost saddle of the main island, and would yield probably less than five gallons a day. The water of both seeps is strongly contaminated with acrid salts, presumably leached from bird droppings.

The birds are as numerous on Necker as on Nihoa and the same species live on both islands except for the Nihoa finch and Nihoa miller bird. The Hawaiian seal has been shot on Necker. Turtles, fish, and crustacea abound.

Palmer (50) states that Necker Island is the remnant of a volcanic cone surrounded by a shoal which marks the position of an adjoining land with an extent of about 650 square miles. Lest the ancient land mass once adhering

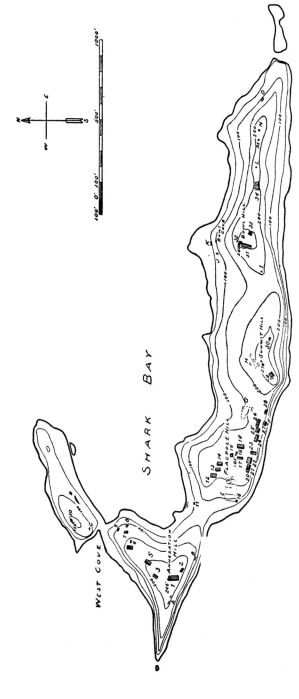

FIGURE 24.—Map of Necker Island showing position of archaeological sites: 1-34, sites of religious structures; *A-O*, sites of other structures. (Topography by Charles S. Judd, contour interval, 50 feet.)

to or in the immediate vicinity of Necker be a convenient place for theorists to establish the home of the Necker people and thus deepen the mystery of the island, and give free reign to speculation, it should be pointed out that the geological evidence shows that Necker Island appears today much as it must have appeared when man is likely to have come upon the scene. The wave cut bench surrounding the island corresponds with that on all the volcanic islands of Hawaii and "appears to be definitely prehistoric."

No evidence of faulting was found on Necker, nor other signs of disturbance which would have resulted from any marked and sudden recent upheavals or sinkings in the neighborhood.

Any violent shock to Necker subsequent to the erection of the rows of uprights on platforms would certainly have toppled over most of the uprights, which are very insecurely fixed, yet more than half are standing, and a third of the fallen ones were evidently knocked down and moved by human agency. (See p. 62.)

HISTORY

La Perouse (30, pp. 473-74), sailing westward, discovered Necker Island, November 4, 1786, and passed close enough to observe its surface features:

It does not exhibit a single tree, but there is a great deal of grass near the summit. The naked rock is covered with the dung of birds, and its white appearance affords contrast to various red spots, upon which the grass has not sprung up. I approached within the distance of a third of a league. The banks were perpendicular, like a wall, and the sea broke so violently against them, that it was impossible to land. As we sailed almost entirely around it, the plan of this island, as well as the different views, are perfectly accurate. I called it *Ile Necker* [in honor of Monsieur Jacques Necker, French Minister of Finance under Louis XVI].

It is stated (23) that Lieutenant J. M. Brooke visited Necker Island some time between January 1 and February 3, 1859 (p. 9). Except that the position of the island was determined, I have found no details of this visit.

The Polynesian (38, August 13, 1859) states that the Hawaiian bark *Gambia* on a sealing and exploring voyage lasting from April 26 to August 7, 1859, visited Necker. No mention is made of landing and according to one paper (35, August 11, 1859), the captain of the *Gambia,* N. C. Brooks, merely reported:

There is a ravine makes down from the southeast end of the rock, where at some seasons there is water. A boat may land in good water at the foot of this gulch.

Documents in the Hawaiian archives (13) relate that in the commission issued to Captain J. A. King by Sanford B. Dole, authorizing him to annex Necker Island in the name of the Provisional Government of Hawaii, the island had been "claimed by the Hawaiian Government since the year 1845, when an expedition under Captain Paty was sent to survey said island."

According to other papers (25, May 31, 1894; 24, June 1, 1894) this statement was repeated in the document read and left on the island. This error was corrected finally in President Dole's proclamation (12) issued June 12, 1894, in which Necker is stated to have been "claimed as Hawaiian territory since 1857, when an expedition was despatched to it by the Hawaiian Government."

It is recorded (28) that in 1857, Captain John Paty, in the schooner *Manuokawai,* was sent by the Hawaiian Kingdom to explore Bird Island, Necker, and other islands to the northwest of the Hawaiian group, and, if it could be accomplished without danger, to land on them, leaving a document saying, "Visited and taken possession of, by order of His Majesty King Kamehameha IV . . ." He was instructed to bring back, besides samples of guano, any curious shells that he might find, with description of their locality. Of the following extracts from the report by Captain Paty (36) the item for April 24 is from his official log, that for April 26 from the original log:

24th April at 6½ P. M. made Necker Island bearing west by south half south, sixteen miles distant. Lay to during the night. At 5½ A. M. filled away, and sailed around the southern side of the Island . . . on some parts small patches of coarse grass were seen. I hove to and tried to catch fish, but not succeeding after spending half an hour's time, I concluded best to proceed on . . . I could not discover any landing place for Boats on the Islet. The surf broke heavy all around it.

26th   At 10 passes within ½ mile around the western side . . . I could not see any inducement to spend any time here, consequently shaped my course for Gardners Island.

Captain William C. Bruhn, of the Inter-Island Steamship Company, says that he landed on Necker about 1879 when he was about 17 years old and a sailor on one of Frank Cooke's schooners, if he remembers rightly, which was the *Julia.*

The ship, on its way to the South Pacific to recruit labor, was becalmed off Necker. He volunteered with some Hawaiians to take a boat and row ashore. His account of their visit, as recorded by Atkinson (2), is here given:

He [Captain Bruhn] went up to the first hill [Annexation Hill] with two of the Hawaiians. He remembers seeing the platforms and says they were just the same in the photographs taken by the Tanager Expedition in 1923, as they were in those days.

From his memory he thinks he saw around him about four or five idols. He picked some of them up and examined them, and wanted to take them on board, but the Hawaiians protested and said it would be sure death to move them. They were so superstitious over them that they didn't bring any on board.

He remembers also seeing a few stone adzes, probably two or three lying around on the ground. They didn't bring any.

Another thing he clearly remembers was a stone shaped like a rough dumbbell, two rough ends with a handle to clutch with the hand. The ends were only roughly hewn but the handle was undoubtedly carved down. The Hawaiians said that when sharks were lured to the shallow places that this dumbbell was used to kill them by beating them on the head. I brought the dumbbell with me and left it in San Francisco.

I can find no mention of this schooner in the shipping list of 1879, but in the Gazette (24, January 17, 1883) the schooner *Julia,* Captain Tierney, is mentioned as having sailed to the Banks and Hebrides groups, in quest of labor for the Planter's Labor and Supply Company, on July 13, 1882, and to have returned, from the Marshall Islands, January 11, 1883.

The ruins and idols of Necker first became known through the accounts of the visit of the party which annexed Necker to the Hawaiian Government in 1894. They believed themselves the first white men to set foot on Necker, the more so because of the discovery of the images and the absence of any signs of earlier foreign visitors.

The Hawaiian steamer *Iwalani,* carrying the annexation party, arrived off Shark Bay, Necker Island, on Sunday morning, May 27, 1894. As published (35, May 30, 1894; 24, June 1, 1894; 25, May 31, 1894), the log of Captain William K. Freeman reads as follows:

> . . . At 11 a. m. arrived at the island and dropped anchor in 18 fathoms of water. We lowered a boat and proceeded to land at once with His Excellency, Capt. J. A. King, Captain Freeman, C. B. Norton [B. H. Norton] and nine sailors, leaving the vessel in charge of the second officer. After considerable difficulty the party was safely landed. A hard climb up a rugged cliff 260 feet high, was successfully accomplished, when His Excellency Capt. King hoisted the Hawaiian flag, read the proclamation and took possession of the island in the name of the Hawaiian Government.
>
> The island is a large lava rock, and was formerly inhabited, as there are square walls about 3 feet high, 4 feet wide, and from 30 to 40 feet long; on the top of which are large flat stones standing on end and set about 2 feet apart. It was first thought that some shipwrecked crew had made a landing here. After a search, however, nothing could be found to indicate that such was the case. Captain Freeman found several old images and idols in a good state of preservation, except for the injuries received by exposure to the weather. A number of these idols were brought back by us as curios. One great curiosity that we found looked like a piece of stone, but, on close inspection, it was thought to be petrified flesh.[3] It was found on a stone altar, and must have been an offering to one of the ancient gods. Birds and fish abounded.
>
> After a stay of about four hours on the island, we left at 5:30 p. m. for home, steering E. by S., arriving at Honolulu on Tuesday evening [May 29].

The following summary of the observations made by the expedition has been published (25, May 31, 1894).

> Nothing of extraordinary interest transpired during the voyage, though the important nature of the expedition, the unusual circumstances necessitating immediate action at Necker Island and the obscurity of the island and dearth of authentic information regarding it, combined to make the cruise of the *Iwalani* one of more than ordinary interest.
>
> Necker Island was found to be an almost sterile heap of volcanic rocks, nearly 300 feet high, but with a few patches of coarse grass on its surface. Upon it, however, distinct traces of human habitation were found. Broken images in stone, sections of stone walls or monuments and the fragments of six well-formed idols were discovered. The idols were brought to Honolulu, set up and placed on exhibition in the windows

---

[3] Fish in a naturally mummified state were seen at several places on Necker by members of the Tanager Expedition. They had been carried there, of course, by birds.

of the Golden Rule Bazaar, where they may be seen today. How long these heathen gods have been on Necker Island, or how long the barren rock was inhabited by man, are problems which must remain unsolved. It would seem plausible, however, that Necker Island was never inhabited for any great length of time. In its sterility but little means of sustenance are offered even to the Polynesians. It is probable some party of natives drifted in the past to Necker Island in open boats, taking these idols with them.

Birds, fish, and turtle were found in abundance, and a few hair seal hang around Necker Island, though these are of little commercial value.

Captain J. A. King said, speaking of the ruins and images (18, June, 1894):

Evidence of the former inhabitants were found in the shape of stone walls, and a small heiau, together with a large number of fragments of small stone idols. Some of the most complete idols were brought away. They materially differ in form and features from the usual style of Hawaiian idols.

Engineer Benjamin H. Norton of the *Iwalani,* and one of the annexation party, had the forethought to take a camera. Seven photographs taken by him, now in the files of Bishop Museum, furnish an invaluable record of the visit. One is reproduced in Plate IX, A; another shows the landing boat anchored off the ledge just west of the beach of Shark Bay. From this point, Captain Norton, in several interviews during September, 1927, has been able to describe to me the movements of all the members of the landing party during the four hours they were ashore, and the circumstances surrounding the discovery and collecting of the images.

In his log Captain Freeman mentions himself as the finder of the images. Captain Norton says he was with Freeman at the time and that the images were collected by both of them and equally divided between them. George N. Wilcox told me that of the four complete images which he presented to Bishop Museum, two were purchased from Captain Freeman and two from Engineer Norton. Also, first officer, James Gregory, present at the flag raising, told me in November, 1927, that after the ceremony Engineer Norton went off with Captain Freeman, while he remained on Annexation Hill with Minister King until the time of departure.

Captain Norton's memory is so clear regarding Necker Island, and his statements in such perfect accord with what was published in the newspapers of that time that I have explicit trust in his statements. He has read and approved my transcription of his account which follows:

Minister King, Captain Freeman, first officer Gregory, three Hawaiian sailors, and myself proceeded from the landing to the gap which almost divides the island in two, and then up the ridge to the summit of the westernmost hill. The remaining [5] sailors, Hawaiians, went fishing and exploring around the coast. On the way up the hill we noticed walls but did not pay particular attention to them, thinking they were geological formations. On top of the hill, however, the largest of these formations was quite evidently artificial, tombstones being set up along the wall. Here we planted the

Hawaiian flag, Minister King read the proclamation with the others around him, while I took a picture of them and the structure (Pl. IX, *A*). After this episode, Minister King and Officer Gregory remained on the hill up to the time of leaving the island, while Captain Freeman and I descended the east slope of the hill to the bottom of the gap between it and the next hill. Then we climbed up the next hill [Flagpole Hill] till we came to the first of several artificial formations. Here we sat down to catch our breath. We were in the middle of the slope and could look out to sea on each side. Above us the ground seemed rather level. I can remember little of the appearance of the ruin where we were sitting because our stay was short and occupied with many other interests. As nearly as I can recall there was a level space about 12 by 15 feet, with a wall running around it except for an opening on one side. The formation was smaller than that where the flagpole had been raised, and seemed better made, but it did not have those tombstones sticking up. We thought of it afterwards as the principal place of worship for the ·island.

From where we were sitting, Freeman and I were idly shying rocks at a bird when he happened to pick up an image fragment. We immediately fell to searching for other pieces, finding plenty. The parts of each idol were close together as if they had been separated only by the weathering which had split them and the disturbance caused by birds continually alighting upon them and pushing pieces to make room for squatting. In the latter manner some pieces had been knocked off the wall on which the idols lay. I do not remember whether these pieces had tumbled within or outside of the inclosure. There was no indication that the idols had been thrown about or broken by human beings. We felt certain we were the first foreigners here.

The idols seemed to have been originally standing but to have fallen on their faces, as we discovered them face down on the wall. They were scattered along over a distance of perhaps 12 feet.

Keeping all the time an anxious eye on the roughening bay, we tried to find all the pieces of each idol we came to. We had gathered together all the pieces of four idols and two or three heads, when we decided we must leave, although many fragments remained, enough, I believe, to have made several other complete images. Putting in our shirts the pieces we had, we hurried to the landing, following the gully which leads to the beach. At the landing we met Minister King and Officer Gregory, who were greatly surprised to learn of the discovery of the idols. At the same moment, three, or possibly four native sailors who were the only members of the party to go along the top of the island further east than Captain Freeman and myself, joined us. One of the natives had a bowl [Pl. XVII, *F*] on his shoulder, the only other stone object collected on the island. They were immediately asked if they had seen idols. They replied to use Norton's exact words, "Oh, yes, they had seen one larger than any of these but it was *aole hanapaa* [not finished, or worked] like them, that it was unfinished and rough."

On board the *Iwalani* I glued together the pieces of each idol as best I could. Captain Freeman and I divided the idols between us, he having the finest idol, another complete idol, and one or two idol heads, and I two complete idols and one head. Captain Freeman also had the stone bowl which the Hawaiian sailors gave him.

I gave my image head to Daniel Balou, my assistant. It is, I am fairly certain, the incomplete idol which was propped up with a jack-knife when the photograph [Pl. XX, *A*] was taken. I do not remember what Captain Freeman did with his image heads, presumably he gave them to others on the boat.

The mention of idols as *aole hanapaa* makes me feel certain that the Hawaiians mistook for an image an uncarved central upright of human form (fig. 26) of which there are two striking examples in the eastern part of the island.

The *H. B. M. S. Champion,* Captain Rooke commanding, landed a party on Necker Island, September 24, 1894. They collected the two images now in the British Museum (Pl. XXII, *A, B*) and the two Atkinson images (Pl. XX, *B*; XXIII, *B*). Nothing more is known of their activities while on the island, but an article (35, October 19, 1894) says "the work done by the *Champion* [in making soundings about Necker] is by this time in the hands of the Canadian Government."

As recorded (24, June 1, 5, and July 12, 1895), Minister King, in the Revenue Cutter *Lehua,* again headed an expedition to Necker Island in 1895 to map the island and to gather up the remaining images. Because of the severe criticism that members of the annexation party had been allowed to privately possess the images collected, a crew composed entirely of Hawaiians was selected for the trip, obviously as they could be relied upon not to take idols. To collect images, birds, and bird eggs, Dr. William T. Brigham, at that time Curator of the Bishop Museum, and an assistant accompanied the *Lehua* expedition. Prof. W. D. Alexander was also on board. The *Lehua* came to anchor off Necker Island at 3:10 a. m., July 12, 1895. The report of Minister King (29) to President Dole reads as follows:

At 6 o'clock a. m. of the same day, we landed and found that the flag pole which we placed in position in May, 1894, had blown down. We replaced the staff in position. We found the Copper Cylinder which had contained the Proclamation open and the document on a rock under the staff. The Proclamation had been opened and a written memorandum in pencil was on the back of it, signed by Officers of the H.B.M. Ship *Champion.* One name I was able to decipher as that of Lieut. Nugent, the others I could not make out. The memorandum stated as near as I can remember as follows: "We, the undersigned officers of the *H.B.M.S. Champion,* on 24th of September 1894, surveyed Necker Island Shoal; running S. E. 35 miles, N. E. 15 miles, and 10 miles in all directions. We found no less than 15 fathoms of water one mile distant from shore."

We returned the Proclamation to the cylinder and made it fast at the base of the staff.

We carefully examined the Island and found no trace of Idols but saw traces of human habitation.

Mr. Dodge, of the Government Survey, made a survey of the Island,[4] and Professor Brigham of the Kamehameha Museum took Photographs of the same, Mr. Brigham also collected a number of specimens of Birds and eggs.

We returned on board the *Lehua* at 2 p. m. on the 12th.

Hon. George N. Wilcox informs me that not long after the discovery of idols on Necker, on two occasions while going out to the leeward islands in quest of guano, he landed on Necker Island, and searched the island from end to end for bowls or idols without finding any.

Elschner (15) records that a few officers and sailors of the U. S. Revenue Cutter *Thetis* swam ashore at Necker in 1910 and that in 1913, the *Thetis* again visited Necker, on which occasion Elschner spent some hours on the

---

[4] The excellent hachure map made by Mr. Dodge shows 5 maraes; Marae 1 and Marae 12, two maraes on the northern ridge of Annexation Hill, and Marae 21 or 22.

island, collecting specimens of basalt, guano, and gypsum. In speaking of the ruins, Elschner states that "idols were found." He does not say when, but it is evident he did not mean that they were found during his visit, else the Bishop Museum would have heard of it.

Mr. H. L. Tucker and party, on an excursion to Necker in 1917, took a large number of photographs, now on file in Bishop Museum, among which are views of Marae 1 and Marae 33. No specimens relating to archaeology were found by them.

Mr. Gerrit P. Wilder as warden of the Hawaiian Islands Bird Reservation, which was created February 3, 1909, visited Necker in the light house tender *Kukui,* on October 6, 1919. While ashore he collected an image leg (Pl. XXIII, *B*) and a reshaped image (Pl. XXIII, *A*), probably the first archaeological objects found on Necker since the visit of the *Champion* in 1894.

The Tanager Expedition first landed on Necker Island at 8:15 a. m., June 12, 1923, and spent four days in topographic mapping under the direction of Charles S. Judd and recording archaeological sites under the direction of Bruce Cartwright. The *Tanager* called again on June 21, and during the stay of several hours, Bowl Cave with its interesting contents was discovered. On June 29, a last visit was paid to Necker, lasting an entire day. These visits resulted in the production of a plane table base map, the recording of most of the maraes, and the collecting of archaeological specimens.

On the morning of July 14, 1924, the Tanager Expedition returned to complete the archaeological survey begun in 1923. Three full days there made possible the recording of the last of the ruins and the satisfactory conclusion of the investigations.

ARCHAEOLOGICAL REMAINS

DISTRIBUTION AND KINDS

The crest of Necker Island is studded with short rows of upright slabs set on low platforms. To a vessel skirting the shore line, many of the uprights are sharply silhouetted against the sky like the teeth of combs. I have called the platforms with their conventional arrangements of uprights "marae," the name by which the structures most nearly resembling them elsewhere in Polynesia are known. These maraes number 33. In contrast to this surprising number, are the few terraces which might have served as cultivation plots or as house platforms. Eight bluff shelters were located. only one of which gave evidence of lengthy occupation.

Maraes

GENERAL REMARKS

The marae ruins of Necker belong to one fixed type from which only 5 out of the 33 maraes vary in any noteworthy degree. The type form is a low, narrow, rectangular platform which faces on a paved rectangular terrace (fig. 25). Along the full length of the rear of the platform an odd number of upright slabs which average 2½ feet in height, 1½ feet in width, and 8 inches in thickness, are set at equal intervals. On the front of the platform a smaller upright stands opposite the central upright. Directly in line with these two, a pair of small uprights are planted on the pavement of

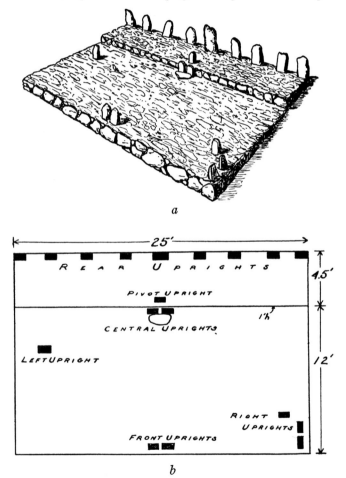

FIGURE 25.—*a,* Sketch (two-point perspective) showing the typical arrangements and most common recurrent dimensions of the marae on Necker Island based on all data available; *b,* plan giving terminology used for uprights.

the terrace and against the platform, at their base a flat slab. Opposite this pair of uprights another pair, or a single upright, stands on the front of the pavement. All these uprights face parallel to the platform.

Viewed from the front, one, two, or three small uprights stand near the right corner of the pavement. Near the left edge of the terrace, about one-third of the way from the platform to the front edge of the pavement, stand one or two small uprights. The right and left terrace uprights face parallel to the platform or at right angles to it.

The platform and terrace is constructed of the unshaped, small and large volcanic stones which lie on the slopes of the island in abundance.. No coral or beach stones were used. The front and side retaining walls of most of the maraes are faced with a single course of rough blocks of stone set on edge. The fill of terrace and platform consists of medium size stones on the bottom, small stones towards the top, and a top dressing or rough pavement of smaller stones.

The following descriptions of marae features cover all maraes of Necker with the exception of five—Maraes 10, 11, 12, 18, and 32—, which are described individually (pp. 67-68), because of their variation from the normal.

PLATFORMS

The platforms range in length from 17.5 feet to 64 feet, but in 16 maraes the length averages close to 25 feet (17.5 to 31 feet), and in 11 maraes, 40 feet (31 to 48 feet).

The width of the platform is 4 to 6 feet in 25 maraes, 3 feet in two, 8 to 9 feet in three. In height the platforms range from 6 to 24 inches above the pavement, and from a few inches to a foot along the back. On very steep or uneven ground the height of the platform naturally varies considerably from one point to another; maximum heights of 5 feet were measured.

Most of the platforms are on the back of the marae terraces, in Maraes 13, 24, and 30 they are on the front. The platforms of Marae 24 and of Marae 30 are exceptional in having a central rearward extension 2 feet deep and 8 feet broad. (See figs. 33 and 35.)

TERRACES

The terraces of the marae are rectangular and occupy all the area directly in front of the platform to a distance not exceeding the platform's length. They rest as low on the ground as possible, since their function is to provide a fairly level quadrangular area before the platform, as is proven by the absence of the terrace in places where the ground is level. Where the level area is large, as in Marae 34, the terrace is merely outlined by a line of stones partly embedded in the ground. The terrace of only one (Marae 9) is surrounded by a wall and this wall is only 4 to 12 inches high.

All artificial terraces and also uneven ground replacing part of the artificial terrace, are roughly paved by laying uppermost the smooth side of the top stones (Pl. XI, *B*). The smooth ground is unpaved.

Because the maraes of Necker rest on steeply sloping and rough ground, terraces and pavements are a constant feature, but on flat land the terrace may not be a platform or even a pavement but instead, a quadrangle marked out by a line of stones embedded in the ground, or by a very rudimentary, low wall, or even by a space cleared of weeds and brush. Such an area might well be called the court of the marae. It should be borne in mind when comparing the Necker Island maraes with ceremonial structures elsewhere, that the very steep slopes limit the outward extension of the court. It is unnecessary to suppose that given extensive horizontal country, these marae builders would keep the court so shortened to the platform.

UPRIGHTS

All uprights are of basalt, the only material locally available. Most of them are rough, weathered, natural blocks; some are dike slabs or prisms; and others are oblong, vesicular, beach stones. No uprights show signs of shaping, except possibly the central rear uprights of Marae 26 and Marae 32. A few uprights appear to have been broken from ledges but by far the most have been selected from talus slopes or the little boulder beach of Shark Bay. The uprights vary from 1 foot to 4 feet, averaging 2½ feet in height. It would require three or four men to carry the largest stones for any distance. (See fig. 26.)

FIGURE 26.—Sketch showing platform, rear, pivot, and central uprights of Marae 26, Necker Island. Marae 27 in the background.
(Drawn from a photograph by E. L. Caum.)

Rear uprights.—The largest of all the uprights are rough, slab-like blocks of lava, set on end along the rear of the platform, insecurely planted in the platform to depths of 3 to 12 inches; of 306 uprights formerly in place, 175 are standing, 74 have fallen, and 57 are missing. Undoubtedly a large number of the uprights no longer standing were knocked over by visitors; others have been blown over by winds. The missing uprights are probably incorporated in other maraes. If this is true, doubtless the maraes were not all built upon one occasion.

On 16 of the 29 maraes the original number of rear uprights is known; on 5 others, only the minimum number. In these 16 maraes, the number ranges from 5 to 21 (5, 7, 9, 11, 13, 19, 21). Two maraes have 7 uprights, five have 9, and five have 11. The platforms with 9 uprights are about 25 feet long, and those with 11 uprights, about 40 feet long, except for Marae 15 in which the platform is only 27.5 feet long.

The central rear upright, that is, the upright having an equal number of uprights on each side, is conspicuously larger than the others in 7 out of the 12 maraes where it could be noted. In the remaining 5 maraes it is of equal size or even smaller. In Marae 26 and Marae 34, the central rear upright, which measures 4 feet high, 2 feet wide, and 2 feet thick, shows a deep front-to-back groove at the top, possibly an artificial notch (fig. 26). Of the other central rear uprights as many are almost flat on top as are definitely pointed.

The rear uprights on each side of the central upright range from 1 to 3½ feet in height, 1 to 2½ in width, 6 to 18 inches in thickness. No special uniformity of shape appears.

FIGURE 27.—Sketch of Marae 33, Necker Island, viewed from the front. (Drawn from a photograph.)

Pivot uprights.—In nine maraes (nos. 3, 14, 21, 23, 24, 26, 31, 33, 34) pivot uprights were noted—two of them black, waterworn stones from the beach (fig. 28), the others lava blocks. They measure 1 to 1½ feet high, 8 to 12 inches wide, and 6 to 8 inches thick. They are planted several inches into the platform and 3 to 12 inches from its front edge.

Irregular platform uprights.—Besides the rear platform and pivot upright, another upright was recorded for one marae. A rough lava upright stands on the middle of the east end of the platform of Marae 27 (fig. 26). It faces inward and appears to have been notched across the top, one side of the notch having broken away.

Central uprights.—Central uprights (fig. 27) made of rough lava blocks, were found on 15 maraes. Nine maraes have pairs of uprights facing the platform in front of the central rear upright; one of these, Marae 34, has a third upright to the left of the pair and nearer the platform. Marae 22 appears to have only this third upright. Five maraes have a single central upright, and its alignment with the central rear uprights of several platforms

a   b

FIGURE 28.—*a*, Sketches of maraes: central uprights of Marae 24; *b*, pivot, central uprights, and slab at the base of the pair of central uprights of Marae 14, Necker Island. (Drawn from photographs.)

indicates that in those maraes, one upright was all that was ever set up. In Marae 5 the central upright is unusually large (3 feet high, 1.5 feet wide), and is placed, not before the middle rear upright, but before the largest rear upright (Pl. X, *B*). All other central uprights vary little in size—1.5 feet high, 1 foot wide, and 8 inches thick. Their shape is more or less rectangular.

In 11 of the 15 maraes where central uprights were observed, one to three flat slabs of lava rock lie in front of the uprights on the pavement at their base. Slabs without uprights in Marae 31 and Marae 33, point to the presence originally of central uprights at these two sites. Only one slab was seen before single central uprights, and also before most of the pairs of uprights. At three places, however, two slabs, and at one place three slabs, are placed before pairs of central uprights. Most of the slabs are roughly oval, with diameters of from 1 to 2½ feet, and a thickness of 5 to 10 inches. Cartwright describes a small, stone-lined chamber under the slab in Marae 1 but I could not verify this nor find such a chamber under any of the other slabs.

The central uprights of Marae 1 and Marae 14 stand on rectangular platforms 6 to 12 inches in height, and not more than 3 feet on a side, which rests against the face of the main platform. Similar small platforms, but without central uprights, were seen at four maraes, an inconspicuous feature possibly overlooked at other maraes.

If these little raised platforms and the stone slabs are indications of the presence of central uprights, then six more maraes, or a total of 21 out of 29, may be said definitely to have had them. The probability is that all of the maraes had them, and that in two-thirds of the maraes they were in pairs, and in the other third, single uprights.

The central upright singles or pairs are placed against the marae platform in six maraes, about 3 inches from the platform in two maraes, and 1 foot away in three maraes.

Front uprights.—Front uprights of the same dimensions and shape as the central uprights were found on 12 maraes. With the exception of one waterworn stone they are all lava slabs. On nine maraes they are in pairs, and three of these (15, 23, 31) have an additional upright. This third upright in Marae 15, a waterworn stone, stands in front of the pair. In Marae 31 it is also in front of the pair, but a little out of line with the other uprights.

On three maraes single front uprights were seen, two of them fairly well aligned with the central uprights, indicating that a single upright may have been all that was intended.

Two pairs of front uprights were not aligned with the central uprights; the pair in Marae 1 was set well to the right, and that in Marae 14, to the left. In two maraes, according to Cartwright, a slab is placed in front of the front uprights.

Front uprights planted 6 inches to 2 feet from the front edge of the terrace pavement are associated with central uprights in all but three maraes, and in these three the presence of the little central platform indicates that central uprights once existed.

Right uprights.—Uprights on the front right corner were noted at 16 maraes. Of these, seven have now, at least, only one right upright; four have two and three have three, one (Marae 31) has four, and one (Marae 20) six. Most of the uprights are lava slabs but a dike prism appears in Marae 21, a beach stone in Maraes 1, 5, and 25, and beach stones form all the uprights of Marae 20. The height of these uprights is 1 to 1½ feet, the width 8 to 16 inches, and the thickness 6 to 12 inches; except for the single, large right upright of Marae 3 and Marae 24, which are 2.5 and 3 feet high, respectively. As may be seen from figure 29, these uprights are arranged in some order. One, two, or three slabs facing inward on the pavement are planted in a row 6 to 12 inches from the right border of the pavement, and near the right corner. In addition, an upright is placed several feet from the right border of the pavement, and 6 inches or, more commonly, 3 to 6 feet from the front. The right uprights of Marae 20 and Marae 34 alone differ from this description (fig. 29).

A flat stone lies on the pavement at the base of the inner face of each of a pair of right uprights of Marae 26 and Marae 34.

The shape of the slab uprights is roughly rectangular; the waterworn uprights are circular in cross section and are round headed.

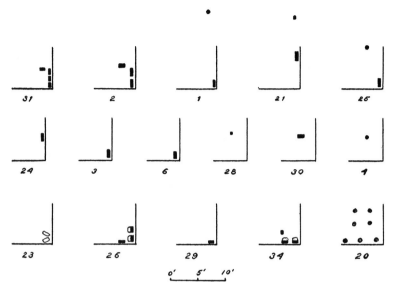

FIGURE 29.—Plans showing the position of the uprights in the right front corner of marae pavements, Necker Island.
(Numbers refer to maraes, fig. 24.)

Left uprights.—On seven maraes are left uprights, all lava slabs; five maraes have one each, and two maraes two each. These uprights average somewhat larger than the right uprights, being 1 to 2½ feet high and proportionately wider and thicker. They are set 3 to 4 feet from the platform and 1 to 2 feet from the left border of the pavement (fig. 30), therefore diagonally opposite the right uprights. As many of them are at right angles to the platform as are parallel with it. No special shape other than a rectangular outline was observed among them.

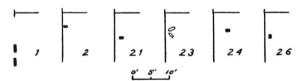

FIGURE 30.—Plans showing position of the uprights on the left rear corner of marae pavements. (Numbers refer to maraes, fig. 24.)

Outside uprights.—At Marae 6 a low, rough platform, 7 by 20 feet, stands 18 feet from the front of the marae, and at right angles to it. In the middle of each end of the platform is a low upright and these are in line with the pair of front uprights of the marae, suggesting of course that the two structures were connected ceremonially.

The variant, Marae 12, has also a low, rough platform, or pavement, placed before the middle of the marae proper. A large upright at the further end of the pavement is directly opposite the entrance uprights (fig. 41).

Marae 14 has an upright placed in the further corner of a pavement 4 feet square, which is attached to the front left corner of the marae terrace. To the left of Marae 9, against the front retaining wall of a tiny adjoining terrace, stand three uprights each about 1 foot high.

VARIANT MARAES

Maraes 10, 11, 12, 18, and 32 differ from the others on Necker Island in several respects: they lack the platform; except for Marae 10, they are enclosed on three sides by a rudimentary wall 6 to 24 inches high; and they differ somewhat from the type form and from each other in the arrangement of uprights. Marae 11 is partly and Marae 12 wholly paved with beach pebbles, the only ones on the island so paved.

a   *b*

FIGURE 31.—*a*, Sketch of Marae 11, viewed from the west; *b*, sketch of right uprights of Marae 34, Necker Island, showing slabs placed at the base of two uprights. (Drawn from photographs.)

These five maraes can not be considered as belonging to one type, unless the common absence of platform is sufficient to establish it as a type. Inspection of plans show Marae 12 more closely related to the usual form than to Maraes 10, 11, 18, or 32. It has identical measurements with the normal maraes, and an even number of uprights on either side of the central rear upright, the equivalent of the pair of central uprights, and a right upright. While employing the main principles of the other maraes, it has its own way of presenting the elements arranged in the median line, and its finish of pavement and central location on the island seem to give it a superiority

(Pl. XII, *A*). I am tempted to ascribe to Marae 12 a slightly different period from those of the type form—a later period rather than an earlier one—if only for the reason that it is one of the best preserved on Necker Island and that the maraes nearest to it, of the normal type, are very much in ruins. It would surely be generally agreed that Marae 12 is of later date than Marae 13, its neighbor, of which but a vestige remains, but of course may not be of later date than all other maraes of the typical form. All the Necker images of human form were discovered at this marae. I attribute these images to the occupants of Bowl Cave, for the reasons set forth on page 118, and it is likely that these people were the last on the island.

Marae 18 and Marae 32 might well belong together. They face east and together cap the summit of a hill. They are about the same size, are enclosed on three sides (not the same three) by walls of the same style. The alignment of their rear uprights links them with those of the common type, but the absence of a platform and the presence of enclosing walls class them with the variants, also certain slight irregularities appear among the uprights. One of the rear uprights of Marae 18 is a dike prism, the only rear upright of this kind seen except in Marae 21 and the irregular Marae 11, and Marae 32 has three small uprights in a row out on the platform. As Marae 34 has three central uprights and Marae 24 appears to have had three, the uprights of Marae 32 may represent the central uprights, though unusually far from the rear ones. Marae 32 is peculiar in having a pit in an extension of the right front corner, possibly the sacred refuse pit such as is associated with Hawaiian and southeastern Polynesian temples. However, this pit may be simply a tiny shelter for protection against the northeast Trade Winds.

Marae 10 also caps the summit of a hill and has its uprights planted directly in the ground. It lacks the enclosing wall which would put it in the same class as Maraes 18 and 32, even though it faces the north.

Marae 11 is the smallest of the five variant temples. It is unlike the other structures except for the presence of uprights orderly arranged along the back and sides. (See figs. 31, *a* and 40.)

BLUFF SHELTERS

A search along the ledges of the bluffs of Necker for places where human beings might have found shelter and left some trace, or where they might have deposited their dead, revealed eight bluff shelters. These are accessible large niches, formed by the weathering out of less resistant lava flows, and identified as shelter sites by means of their artificially terraced floors in which, at all but two (Sites B and C), ashes, beach pebbles, or cooking stones were observed. Of the niches in the bluffs, high above the dash of spray and quite suitable for shelter, there are probably not more than twelve.

These bluff shelters were the only unmistakable dwelling or camping sites discovered on Necker Island. Only one, where a large number of artifacts were found, gave evidence of continuous occupation. Buried in the floor of this shelter were the leg bones of an individual. This might well be interpreted as a reburial, but an equally acceptable interpretation is that these bones were taken to the shelter to be manufactured into fishhooks or other objects. In Hawaii leg bones were highly prized for fishhook material.

The mouths of the bluff shelters are 10 to 70 feet long, but the width of the ledge protected by the overhang reaches a maximum at each shelter of only about 5 feet. Site F is unusual in having an overhang of 12 feet. The terrace covers the entire floor of the niche in all but three shelters. The retaining walls consist of a single line of stones, the surface covered with at least several inches of cave dust.

The capacity of some bluff shelters is but one person, others as many as six. Allowing an average of three, it might be said with much justification that 24 people are all that could be sheltered at one time by the eight grottos.

Most puzzling is the occurrence of several dike prism uprights on the back part of the floors of Shelters D and F. I suggest that these may be bird tethers rather than shrines as they have no regular arrangement, and as no more suitable purpose occurs to me. Along the south bluff of Annexation Hill, at the same level as Shelter B, I saw single uprights in several niches about 1.5 feet wide, high, and deep. Tropic birds were nesting behind them. On Nihoa such dike prism uprights are at bluff shelter Site 23, and what may be fallen uprights at Sites 48 and 60. A dike upright stands at the entrance to Shelter O, Necker.

Though all bluff shelters were excavated, Bowl Cave alone yielded artifacts.

Terraces

I counted 25 terraces on Necker, arranged in five groups distributed as follows: two small, separate terraces just west of the summit of Annexation Hill; one group of a series of 8 terraces in a swale south of Flagpole Hill; a group of 6 terraces in the saddle between Flagpole Hill and Summit Hill; a group of 7 terraces just northwest of the crest of Summit Hill; and a double terrace adjoining Marae 29, on the same hill. These sites occupy ground which is the most level and which is covered with some of the deepest soil.

The terraces are quadrangular, unpaved, low, and, with some exceptions, narrow. There is a total absence of walls on or about them. The retaining walls are characteristically of single course construction. In the best of them the stones are set on edge with the largest and flattest surface vertically exposed. Soil and gravel cover the front of the terraces but do not exceed a depth of 3 or 4 inches. There is evidence in the vertical projection of the retaining walls at the lower terrace of Site H (Pl. XIII, *B*) and at the double terrace adjoining Marae 29 (Pl. XIII, *A*) of a former greater depth of soil which has been removed by water and wind.

The height of the terraces is 6 inches to 2 feet, with one terrace (Site G) 4 feet high. The width, that is, the level area back of the retaining walls, is 5 or 6 feet in most terraces, but the range is 4 to 15 feet. The most common length is 20 to 30 feet; the range is 9 to 60 feet.

Not a single artifact was found on any of the terraces although each site was searched more than once and the shallow surface soil combed.

One or two terraces in each group have the appearance of house sites. They are wide, level, and free of loose stones lying on the surface, and have room for houses 5 by 10 feet or 10 by 15 feet, about the size of the houses at the ancient fishing village of Kaunolu, Lanai, which I estimated as 6.5 by 15.5 feet (17, p. 44). However, there is no evidence that the terraces were used as house sites. Household possessions, bones, shells, and oven stones are lacking. They may, of course, have been removed but it is incredible that such a hunt as was conducted by the Tanager Expedition would have yielded not one object had the terraces been occupied as dwelling sites for any length of time.

To consider all the 25 terraces as dwelling sites presents the problem of cultivation sites, as much of the soil covered area of the island is contained in these terraces.[5] On the other hand, if all terraces are regarded as gardens, some place must be found for the inhabitants. The eight dwelling caves might have sheltered a maximum of 25 people but only Bowl Cave in which four or five could have lived gives any proof of prolonged habitation. Perhaps ten people living on the island would have needed all the agricultural terraces. If houses or shelters were erected on the island, it may be assumed that their sites would be marked by a terrace, because the Necker islanders were terrace builders and everywhere the ground was rough and steep. Certain of the terraces which appear too carefully made for garden terraces and which are covered with too shallow a soil to grow crops, may have been dwelling sites. If the dwellings were built of local materials they must have been huts constructed of a few sticks of drift wood and the branches of bushes, and thatched with leaves or grass. There is space, however, for houses of fair size. Timbers well may have been imported.

Terraces like the lower ones west of Flagpole Hill and northwest of Summit Hill, stretch widely across the swales and hold their surface soils

---

[5] In C. H. Judd's notes he tells of sowing seed in the swale between Summit and Bowl hills "where the most soil is found, and this but scanty." No terraces were found there.

from washing away, therefore suggesting that they were intended to pocket soil in which to raise crops of sweet potato, sugar-cane, or such food plants.

It seems to me that not more than ten terraces could possibly be interpreted on the basis of their appearance as house or dwelling sites, one at Site A, four at Site E, one at Site G, two at Site H, and two at Marae 29. Were all these so occupied, 15 terraces would be left for cultivation.

PLATFORMS

Along the crest of Bowl Hill are four low platforms or pavements, 5 to 10 feet square. The westernmost is a pavement of beach boulders and hence seems to have a ceremonial character; the others are very rough pavements, perhaps nothing more than observation stations (p. 90).

ARCHAEOLOGICAL SITES

MARAES

Each ruin is located, drawn to scale, and oriented on the map of Necker Island (fig. 24). The maraes are numbered consecutively from west to east; and the other sites are lettered.

The following descriptions of maraes are largely dependent upon their plans. The few conventions used are explained in figure 32. As most of

FIGURE 32.—Key to symbols used on marae plans.

the uprights are shown in the field photographs, I have given their outline in as far as this source of information would permit.

By taking Cartwright's record of 22 maraes into the field, I was able to identify and locate them and to check at least the main features. The members of the Expedition responsible for the original plans are designated as follows: Cartwright (C), Caum (L), Emory, assisted by Hanson (E); some of the original plans were checked and slightly modified by me. With the exception of Maraes 8, 10, 13, and 20, photographs of the maraes are on file in Bishop Museum.

Marae 1. (CE; fig. 33 and Pls. IX, *A*, and X, *A*.) The largest and evidently the principal rear upright is no. 9, whereas from observations of the other maraes, no. 10 would be expected. Upright 9, by tape measurements, stands exactly midway between the ends of the platform.

It is interesting to examine the photographs taken at this marae in 1894 (Pl. IX, *A*), which show uprights nos. 1 to 16, as they were in 1924, except upright no. 8, which was not standing. A photograph taken by H. L. Tucker in 1917 shows this upright standing. This marae is the most likely to be visited by all landing parties, and its condition today compared to thirty years ago seems to speak well for the treatment the maraes have received by the later visitors. However, between 1923 and 1924, photographs prove that

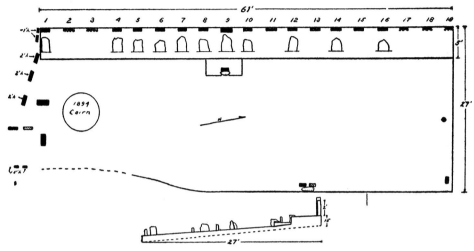

FIGURE 33.—Plan of Marae 1, Necker Island, and side elevation as viewed from the north; 2'h and other figures indicate height.

at least three uprights of Marae 5 have been knocked down, and one upright pushed to a leaning position.

The uprights to the left of the marae proper stand on level ground. If they belong to this structure they present an irregularity not found elsewhere among the maraes, and if they are the remains of another marae, which I think is more probable, they are to be understood only by considering the five uprights as rear uprights. It will be noted that Maraes 20 and 21 meet each other at right angles, so that a marae joining Marae 1 at right angles would not be unique.

Figure 33 shows the plan as checked and corrected by Lieut. E. J. Brown, Coast and Geodetic Survey, who visited Necker in June, 1928.

Marae 2. (C; fig. 34.) Except for the extreme left rear upright which I noted as missing, nothing is known of the other uprights except that some have fallen. The two central uprights marked "on edge" undoubtedly supported a slab thus forming a small chamber, unless the space between these two stones was filled in, forming a little platform such as may be seen in Maraes 14, 22, and 31. The line of the front edge of the terrace is determined by the topography.

In response to my request, Lieut. E. J. Brown kindly checked this plan on the spot in June, 1928, and reported that all uprights are as shown except the 2nd, 4th, and 7th rear uprights, which are fallen.

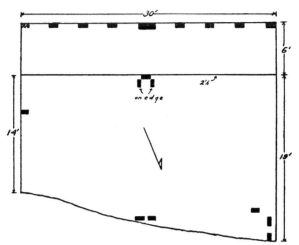

FIGURE 34.—Plan of Marae 2, Necker Island. (For key to symbols see fig. 32.)

Marae 3. (EL; fig. 35.)

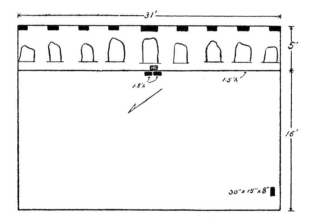

FIGURE 35.—Plan of Marae 3, Necker Island. (For key to symbols see fig. 32.)

Marae 4. An independent and slightly differing plan of Marae 3, by Cartwright, and one which was located a few feet further north than the plan by Caum, was at first thought to be another marae, which I designated as Marae 4. However, Lieut. E. J. Brown, by going to the spot in June, 1928, determined that both plans represent the same ruin.

Marae 5. (E; fig. 36 and Pl. X, *B*.) Most of the front of the marae is the bare slope of a hill. The marae is bounded along the front by a retaining wall a foot high. Lieut. E. J. Brown has verified the plan.

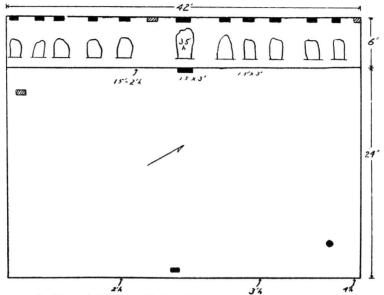

FIGURE 36.—Plan of Marae 5, Necker Island. (For key to symbols see fig. 32.)

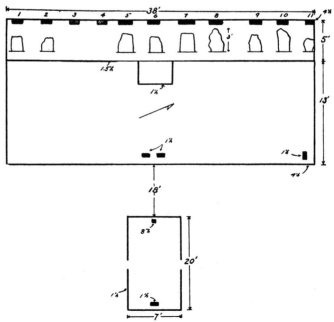

FIGURE 37.—Plan of Marae 6, Necker Island. (For key to symbols see fig. 32.)

Marae 6. (CE; fig. 37.) It is clear that the central rear upright of this marae is one of the smaller uprights.

Marae 7. (CE; fig. 38, *a*.) The front of the platform is bounded by an outcrop of large rocks, which are connected by the front retaining wall. This accounts for the curved front of the marae.

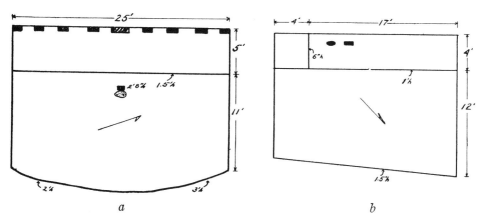

a   *b*

FIGURE 38.—Plans of maraes, Necker Island: *a*, Marae 7; *b*, Marae 8. Lieut. E. J. Brown says the fourth rear upright of Marae 7 is missing and the fifth and ninth are fallen. (For key to symbols see fig. 32.)

Marae 8. (C; fig. 38, *b*.) This structure is in very poor condition. Only the two uprights are standing, that on the extreme left a black, water-worn stone.

Marae 9. (E; fig. 39, *a*.) As the boundaries of this marae are indefinite, the plan is only approximate. The uprights are about 2 feet high. Seven of them stand on main platform, and a slab, probably a rear upright, lies in the position shown. A rudimentary wall a few inches high bounds

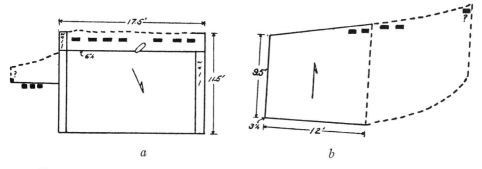

a   *b*

FIGURE 39.—Plans of maraes, Necker Island: *a*, Marae 9; *b*, Marae 10. (For key to symbols see fig. 32.)

the marae on each side. Adjoining on the east is a small terrace with three uprights about a foot high placed against its retaining wall. A stone a few inches high and set on end is incorporated in the left corner of the retaining wall.

Marae 10. (E; fig. 39, *b*.) In extremely poor condition. The boundaries are indefinite. The left half is marked out by stones embedded in the ground. The right half is not paved. The dotted line (fig. 39, *b*) enclosed the area cleared of rough stones. The uprights are a foot or less in height. There is no indication of a platform.

Marae 11. (CE; figs. 40 and 31, *a*.) At the very base of the steep slope into Shark Bay are these two tiny adjoining terraces. The terrace on the left was paved with beach pebbles. The high, rough retaining wall was taken down and the terrace completely excavated without discovering artifacts. Just outside the southwest corner Cartwright noted 5 flat, beach stones, 1 foot long, set on their sides.

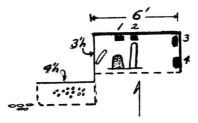

FIGURE 40.—Plan of Marae 11, Necker Island. (For key to symbols see fig. 32.)

Around the ends of the outer border of the right terrace runs a wall a foot high consisting of a single course of stones. Upright no. 1 is a black stone, upright no. 2 a dike slab, uprights nos. 3 and 4 are waterworn stones 1 foot and 1.5 feet high, respectively.

Marae 12. (CE; fig. 41 and Pl. XII, *A*.) The floor is paved with beach pebbles 1 to 2 inches in diameter. The central rear upright is supplanted by a small pointed slab, and on each side of it a smaller, black, beach stone set upright. This looks phallic. The central pair of uprights are placed immediately before the central rear upright and in line with the other rear uprights. The remains of what seems to have been a small compartment formed of flat stones set on edge are found a few feet in front of the central uprights. This may have been filled with small stones to form a little platform.

The front of the marae is on a level with the outside ground and is marked off simply by a line of stones embedded in the ground.

The large upright outside of the marae proper and in direct line with the central uprights, is 2.5 feet high, 1.5 feet thick, and 2 feet wide. It stands on the outer edge of a rectangular pavement adjoining the marae, perfectly vertical, and presenting its flat face towards the marae. The pavement which is not more than 4 inches thick, rests on solid rock.

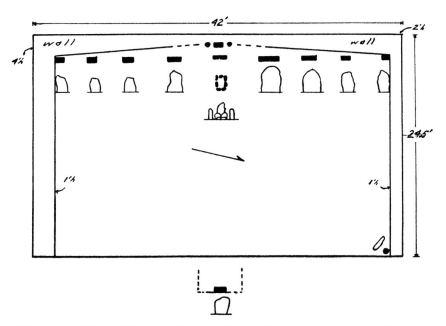

FIGURE 41.—Plan of Marae 12, Necker Island.   (For key to symbols see fig. 32.)

The unfinished image (Pl. XXIII, *D-F*) was found 8.5 feet west of the southwest corner, and the fragment of leg, a few feet away partly covered by pigweed.

Marae 13.   (C.)   A rough platform 25 feet wide on the down hill side, 22 feet wide on the up hill side, and 27 feet at each end.   Across the down hill side is a platform 9 feet wide and a foot high.   No uprights are on this, but in the rear left (southwest) corner of the terrace and against the platform is a large upright.   This is the only left upright that is not several feet from the platform.   Possibly Cartwright is mistaken in giving a width of 9 feet to the platform.   If the width of the platform were the usual 6 feet, then the upright would be the usual 3 feet from it.

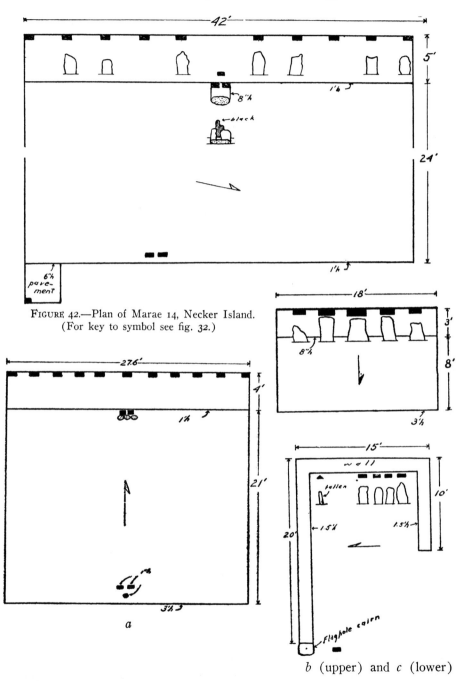

FIGURE 42.—Plan of Marae 14, Necker Island.
(For key to symbol see fig. 32.)

b (upper) and *c* (lower)

FIGURE 43.—Plans of maraes, Necker Island: *a*, Marae 15 uprights shown as standing, though several are fallen; *b*, Marae 16; *c*, Marae 18. (For key to symbols see
fig. 32.)

Marae 14. (CE; figs. 42, 28, *b.*) The central rear upright, if ever present, is now missing. The upright on the corner of the little pavement adjoining the marae is small.

Marae 15. (C; fig. 43, *a.*) The records do not state whether or not the rear uprights are standing. The central upright is broken.

Marae 16. (C; fig. 43, *b.*) Along the rear of the platform and forming the retaining wall is a wall a foot high consisting of a single course of stones set on edge.

Marae 17. (C.) Twenty by 40 feet, facing west. The northwest corner is 6 feet west of the summit cairn. The platform, which is in fair condition, is 6 feet wide. Most of the 9 rear uprights have fallen. The terrace is almost entirely unpaved, only its outline being preserved.

Marae 18. (C; fig. 43, *c* and Pl. X, *C.*) The floor is the level summit of the hill top.

Marae 19. (C; fig. 44.) The terrace is mainly the bare slope of the hill, which is quite steep.

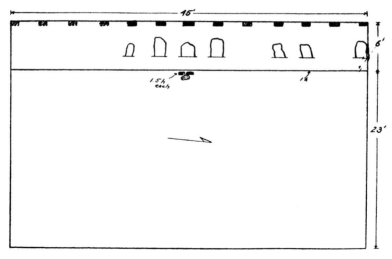

FIGURE 44.—Plan of Marae 19, Necker Island. (For key to symbols see fig. 32.)

Marae 20. (C; fig. 45, *b.*) The number of uprights which have fallen is not recorded. A distant photograph proves that most of them are standing. The north corner of the terrace is broken down. In the west corner are six waterworn stones 6 inches in diameter and a foot high, which, if standing, probably would have the positions given. Only one, however, stands. Two lava slabs lie close by. Marae 20 joins Marae 21 at right angles.

Marae 21. (C; fig. 45, *a* and Pl. X, *D.*) The presence of three 8-inch square, flat, waterworn black slabs embedded where shown on the terrace, is an oddity. The remains of a little platform of a single course of slabs is placed against the platform and before the pivot upright.

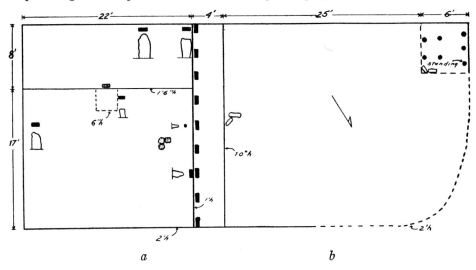

FIGURE 45.—Plan of maraes, Necker Island: *a,* Marae 21; *b,* Marae 20. (For key to symbols see fig. 32.)

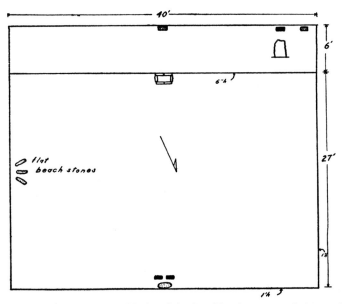

FIGURE 46.—Plan of Marae 22, Necker Island. (For key to symbols see fig. 32.)

Marae 22. (C; fig. 46.) Separated by six feet of level bed rock from Marae 21. Rear uprights other than those indicated have been knocked down and moved from their original location. Placed centrally against the platform is a small, lower platform with retaining walls of six or seven small stones set on edge. On the left side of the terrace, Cartwright notes three flat beach stones set flush with the pavement.

Marae 23. (CE; fig. 47.) Much in ruins. The south boundaries are indefinite. The court is level, unpaved ground. The platform is rough and uneven, only two uprights stand. Cartwright estimates 13 rear uprights and reports the pivot upright as rounded, the central uprights as flat, and all standing. I found them fallen. At the location of the front upright, six loose waterworn stones lay on the front of the marae court. One of the two fallen uprights on the left edge of the marae has a natural hole in the side, 2 inches in diameter.

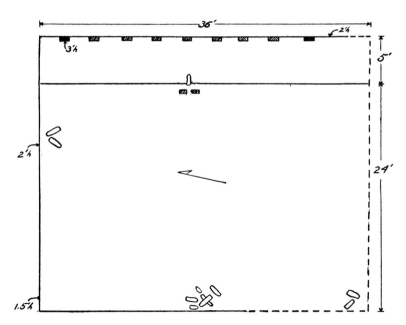

FIGURE 47.—Plan of Marae 23, Necker Island. (For key to symbols see fig. 32.)

Marae 24. (E; fig. 48, Pl. XI, *A*.) The back is on the edge of the sea bluff and is supported by a retaining wall 4 feet high. The court is level, smoothly paved, and merges into the hill slope but its boundary is marked by a line of stones embedded in the ground. The fallen upright lying back of the central rear upright is a black, waterworn stone about 2 feet long. Two fallen rear uprights to the east of the central rear uprights are given in their probable original position. Other uprights must have tumbled over

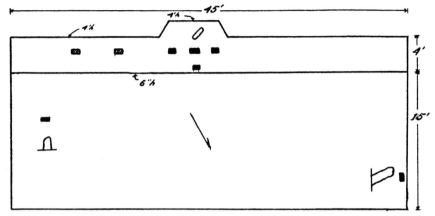

FIGURE 48.—Plan of Marae 24, Necker Island. (For key to symbols see fig. 32.)

the bluff. The large right upright showing in Plate XI, *A* was fallen a year later in 1924.

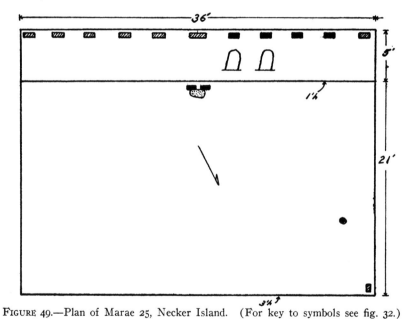

FIGURE 49.—Plan of Marae 25, Necker Island. (For key to symbols see fig. 32.)

Marae 25. (E; fig. 49.) The central rear upright and all those to the east of it are fallen forward on the platform. Half a foot from the front of the platform are the two central uprights tilted away from the platform. No chamber is beneath the slab placed at the base of the central uprights.

Marae 26. (CE; figs. 26 and 50.) The pavements of the platform and of the terrace, as in most maraes, are not horizontal but dip with the hill slope. The body of the central rear upright is very suggestive of the human form. There is a V-shaped notch, 6 inches deep, in the top. The notch may be artificial but I could discover no clear traces of shaping. Marae 34 also has

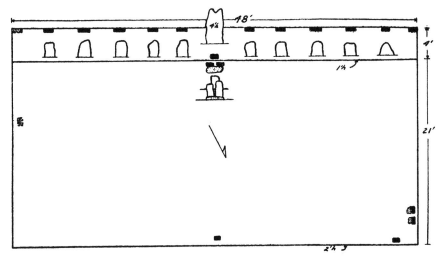

Figure 50.—Plan of Marae 26, Necker Island. (For key to symbols see fig. 32.)

a central rear upright with a similar notch, making it seem probable that both were purposely so shaped. Weathering might well have obliterated tool marks.

Marae 27. (CE; figs. 51, *a* and 26.) A very rough ruin on a steep slope. The unusual platform upright on the left has a prong and appears to have had two, forming a notch resembling that in the central rear uprights of Maraes 26 and 34. The pronged upright was standing in 1923 but was lying flat in 1924. One rear upright was observed lying on the edge of the sea bluff just back of the marae.

Marae 28. (E; fig. 51, *b*.) The two gaps in the row of the rear uprights would have allowed for three more uprights, forming then a chain of 11 uprights placed 1.5 to 2 feet apart.

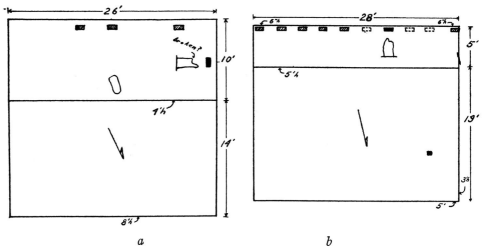

a   b

FIGURE 51.—Plans of maraes, Necker Island: *a*, Marae 27; *b*, Marae 28. (For key to symbols see fig. 32.)

Marae 29. (E; fig. 52; Pl. XIII, *A* for adjoining terrace.)   The terrace adjoining the marae on the right is divided into two levels differing by 6 inches.   Both are filled evenly with soil and small, rough pebbles.   The

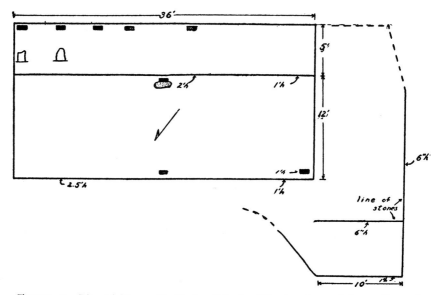

FIGURE 52.—Plan of Marae 29, Necker Island. (For key to symbols see fig. 32.)

retaining walls are a single line of stones set on edge. The marae rises a foot higher than the terrace.

Marae 30. (E; fig. 53.) The platform as well as the terrace pavement is rough and uneven. The front retaining wall of the terrace is solidly built though of large, extremely irregular rocks.

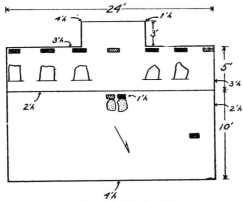

FIGURE 53.—Plan of Marae 30, Necker Island. (For key to symbols see fig. 32.)

Marae 31. (E; fig. 54; Pl. XI, *B*.) Measurement with cloth tape determined that the central upright of this long line of rear uprights was located within 6 inches of the exact center. The tiny platform set against the main platform is bordered by small slabs set on edge and is filled with stones and gravel on which is set a flat stone.

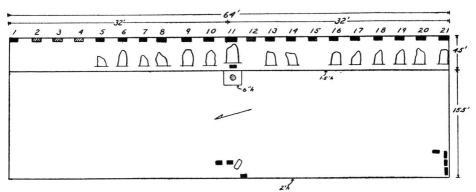

FIGURE 54.—Plan of Marae 31, Necker Island. (For key to symbols see fig. 32.)

Marae 32. (E; fig. 55, *a*.) The platform is indicated by a raise of only 3 inches from the floor of the marae. The partly enclosing wall is 1.5 to 2 feet high.

Built in the front right corner of the terrace is an enclosure 3 by 6 feet, broken down or left open on the southwest. The back wall of the enclosure and the north wall are the vertical retaining walls of the terrace, 2 to 3 feet high. The enclosure may be looked upon as a rock shelter, or as the sacred refuse pit of the marae.

Marae 33. (E; figs. 55, *b* and 27.)

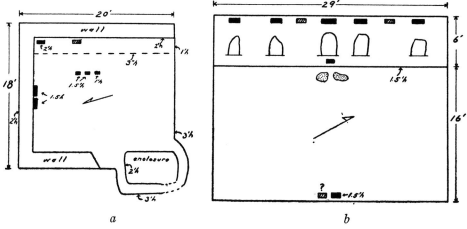

a　　　　　　　　　　　　*b*

FIGURE 55.—Plans of maraes, Necker Island: *a*, Marae 32; *b*, Marae 33. (For key to symbols see fig. 32.)

Marae 34. (L; fig. 56.) Entirely straddles the island ridge which is flat at this point. The central rear upright which is fallen forward, is 3.5 feet long and the upper end notched as with the central rear upright of Marae 26. (See also fig. 30, *b*.)

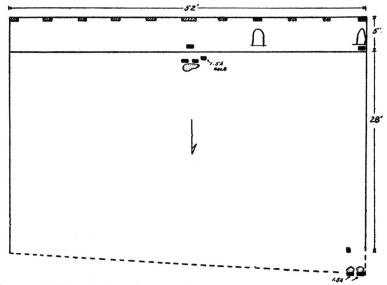

FIGURE 56.—Plan of Marae 34, Necker Island. (For key to symbols see fig. 32.)

Sites Other than Maraes

Site A. Two indistinct terraces on the edge of a sheer drop to the sea. Both are 5 feet wide with a retaining wall a foot or less in height. The terrace on the west is 19 feet long, that on the east, 9 feet.

Site B. Bluff shelter. A ledge 39 feet long and 15 feet wide sheltered for about 8 feet by the overhang of the bluff. Against the back of the shelf and between the ends is a terrace 3.5 by 6 feet, and a foot high. The retaining walls are a single course of stones.

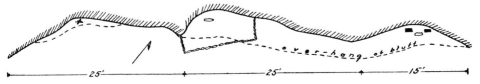

FIGURE 57.—Plan of Site D, Necker Island.

Site C. A bluff shelter having a rough terrace similar in size and shape to that at Site B. Excavated but no artifacts found.

Site D. A bluff shelter (fig. 57) located on a shelf 70 feet long and 3 to 10 feet wide. Against the back of the shelf and about midway from the ends is a rough terrace 6 by 12 feet. A dike prism lies on the terrace. Near the back wall of the southern end lie several dike splinters, and a beach pebble. Near the back wall of the northern end are two uprights about a foot in height and a dike splinter lying flat between them.

Site E. Series of terraces (fig. 58; Pl. XII, B). Across the lower end

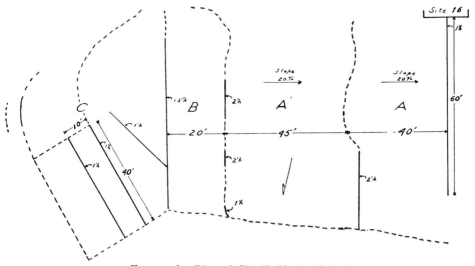

FIGURE 58.—Plan of Site E, Necker Island.

of the swale west of Flagpole Hill are four long, narrow terraces; and across the upper end four smaller terraces. The retaining walls are a single line of stones 6 inches to 2 feet in height. In the lower four terraces the amount of level, cleared ground immediately back of the front retaining walls is only 3 to 6 feet wide. In the upper four terraces it is wider.

Site F. A bluff shelter discovered by Edward L. Caum (fig. 59). This shelter is 30 feet below the top of the bluff. A low retaining wall has been built across the mouth of this grotto and the floor roughly filled in and

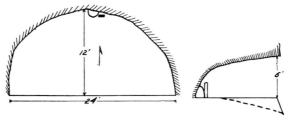

FIGURE 59.—Plan of Site F, Necker Island.

paved with rubble. Digging into this floor revealed no artifacts. At the very back of the shelter a rock about 2 feet in diameter has been placed, and next to it an upright.

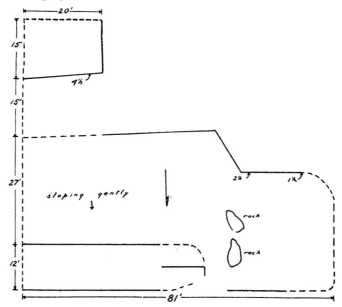

FIGURE 60.—Plan of Site G, Necker Island.

Site G. Group of six terraces in the flat north swale of the col between Flagpole Hill and Summit Hill (fig. 60). The highest terrace is 4 feet high, 10 feet wide, and 20 feet long, and looks like a house site. The other terraces are very low, partly bounded by single lines of stones, and for the most of their length, barely traceable. The area is almost free of loose, scattered stones. A long search over the shallow surface soil of this area revealed no artifacts.

Site H. A group of seven terraces (fig. 61). The highest terrace, 12 by 24 feet, has the dimensions and the appearance of a house site. The lowest terrace also (Pl. XIII, *B*) appears to be a dwelling site. A shelf 25 to 30

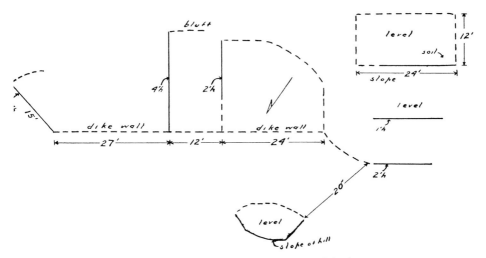

FIGURE 61.—Plan of Site H, Necker Island.

feet broad, running around the northwest side of Summit Hill, near the top, bears the other five terraces. A low dike wall bounds them on the north and a bluff on the south. A sprinkling of soil lies on parts of all the terraces.

Site I. A pavement 6 feet square made of a single course of large water-worn oval stones having long diameters of 1.5± feet and short diameters 1± foot.

Site J. A bluff shelter 15 feet wide, 9 feet deep in the middle. Thorough excavating resulted in only three beach pebbles. The extreme depth of soil on the floor was 8 inches.

Site K. A bluff shelter 30 feet wide, 5 feet deep. Six inches was the maximum depth of soil on the floor, which was mostly bare ledge. Excavation revealed two beach pebbles 2 by 4 inches in diameter and two, 4 by 8 inches in diameter. Ashes of a fire were unearthed in the middle of the floor.

Bowl Cave. A bluff shelter 15 feet long, 8 feet wide, and with a roof high enough to permit a person to stand upright. The floor is terraced and the depth of soil (30 inches) is greater than that found at any other bluff shelter.

Bowl Cave is accessible from the west by means of a narrow ledge, along which and a few feet from the shelter is the largest of the two seeps on the island. Palmer (37) thought it would be possible to collect 5 gallons of water a day from this seep. The water, however, is at present "highly contaminated with acrid salts, presumably leached from bird droppings."

William Anderson, upon discovering the bluff shelter, saw the tip of a boat-shaped bowl (Pl. XIX, *F*) right-side-up sticking out of the floor at the west end. Six days later Anderson and Wilson unearthed a bird-snaring perch (Pl. XV, *E*), remnants of two bowls, and 3 crude basalt adzes.

Later, nearly all of the scientific personnel of the first Tanager Expedition took some part in the complete excavation of the shelter, and screening of the material. The additional objects found include six adzes, one chisel, one adz reject, one hammerstone, three sinkers, one stone awl, numerous beach pebbles, a fragment of *wiliwili* wood, and the right and left femurs and tibia of a human skeleton.

Sites L, M, and N. Three platforms or pavements made of a single course of rough stones averaging a foot in diameter. Each pavement takes up the width of the ridge at the point of its location. Site L is 5 by 6 feet. Site M is somewhat septigonal, with its greatest width, 10 feet, and its smallest width, 6 feet. Site N is 10 feet square.

Site O. A bluff shelter (fig. 62). The floor is terraced. The eastern end is enclosed by a low wall in which many of the stones are dike slabs placed upright. A dike upright stands on the ledge leading to the cave from

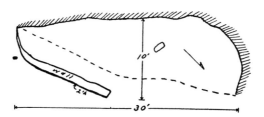

FIGURE 62.—Plan of Site O, Necker Island.

the east. On the floor of the terrace lay a beach stone a foot long and half a foot in diameter. Though this large shelter gave promise of a fruitful yield of artifacts if excavated, the careful sifting of the 6 inches of dust on the floor brought no specimens.

ARCHAEOLOGICAL SPECIMENS

IMPLEMENTS FROM BOWL CAVE

HAMMERSTONE

One shaped hammerstone (fig. 63, *a*), both ends of which reveal much battering, was collected in Bowl Cave. The sides have been shaped by chipping off great flakes along the grain of the dike rock. A thumb hold has been chipped out of one side.

a　　　　　　　　*b*　　　　　　　　*c*

FIGURE 63.—Artifacts from Bowl Cave, Necker Island: *a*, hammerstone length 2.5 inches, weight 5 ounces; *b*, adz block 2.1 inches long, 0.9 inches wide, 0.45 inches thick, weight 1 ounce, showing highly polished side; *c*, retouched splinter of basalt, probably an awl, length 3.5 inches.

GRINDSTONES

Two slightly worn grindstones were unearthed in the same strata as the adzes. One is a roughly square piece of gray dike prism, 8 by 8 inches and 2 inches thick, with a flat face worn smooth by grinding. The grain is so fine that grit must have been used to assist in any grinding of stone implements. Such scratches as are traceable are parallel. The other grindstone is a somewhat vesicular slab of blue-gray basalt that had been taken from a beach where erosion had developed the forms described by Wentworth (49) as chink-facets, which might be taken for artificial shaping. It is roughly a square 11 by 11 inches, and 3 inches thick. Both faces are worn smooth and a trifle concave by grinding. The grit is much coarser than that of the other stones. It is quite likely that the two stones were used in conjunction since the coarser grained stone, which naturally would be used for the preliminary grinding, has received the greater wear. Neither stone has had excessive wear.

The large grindstone is suitable for a platter, or as a nether grinder in the preparation of food and may have been so used. There is no doubt in my mind that it was employed also in grinding and shaping the stone implements found in the cave.

ADZES, CHISEL, AND AWL

Of the seven adzes from Bowl Cave, six show careful shaping and grinding, and one is extremely crude. They were found in sifting the floor dirt through a screen, hence it is now impossible to tell whether the crude

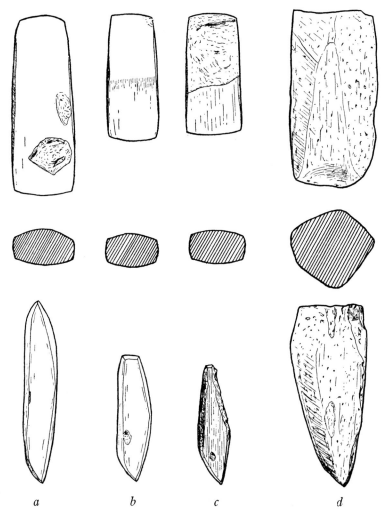

a	*b*	*c*	*d*

FIGURE 64.—Front view, cross section at angle of blade with tang, and profile of adzes from Bowl Cave, Necker Island: *a*, double bitted adz or adz-ax; *b*, adz; *c*, fractured adz; *d*, blade of rough adz.

adz belonged to a different level, or if the finished adzes were grouped together as a single cache, or lay scattered on the "living" floor.

See Table 3 for weights and measurements.

The ground adzes are of compact basalt. The largest two are red-gray, probably from having been in the fire; the others are blue-black. They have been shaped by chipping and excessive grinding on all surfaces; no pecking work is visible. All but the largest chip marks are entirely ground out, leaving the adz smooth to the touch. The cross section is a rectangle slightly convex on the sides and a little more so on the top and bottom. The width of the poll and of the cutting edge are nearly the same, but the width of the middle of the adz is greater. The sides and the front are convex longitudinally, but the front longitudinal curve is not single for the curve of the blade and the curve of the tang meet at a distinct angle which forms a ridge visible on all adzes except the largest, in which the juncture shows in the front longitudinal margins. The back of the adz is slightly concave longitudinally except the adzes shown in figure 64, *c*.

The bevel of the bit emerges imperceptibly into the back in four adzes, but leaves a line of demarkation, or chin, in one (fig. 64, *c*). The edge is convex viewed from above, but straight in the face view. The poll is convex or flat. In place of a poll the largest adz (fig. 64, *a*) is remarkable in having the bit of an axe.

The adz shown in fig. 64, *c* appears to have a pronounced tang, it therefore should be noted that a fracture, subsequent to its finishing, has removed the larger part of the front.

Weights and measurements of five of the adzes are given in Table 3. The sixth adz is represented by a fragment of blade showing only a completely ground surface on front and back, a thickness of at least .7 inches and a width of at least 1.2 inches.

Mingled with the floor dust of the bluff shelters are many fragments and splinters of dike rock which could have come from the weathering of the floor, roof, or sides of the shelter. Some of these pieces having sharp edges were picked up as artifacts but, on showing no trace of working, discarded. However, a crudity from Bowl Cave roughly of the form of a small, tanged adz, rectangular in cross section, bears an unmistakable, ground, convex bevel (fig. 65, *d*). The cutting edge is badly nicked. The suspicion is aroused by this specimen that some of the adz-shaped, entirely natural fragments with a keen edge were actually used. Two of these 2.2 and 3 inches in length, respectively, were collected from Bowl Cave; one bears a few chip marks which may or may not have been artificial.

A roughly chipped blade portion of an unfinished large adz was collected (fig. 64, *d*). The cross section of the blade is triangular, the base of the triangle forming the front. The sides are parallel. The cutting edge is convex from the view above and the view in front. The bevel is concave near the edge.

What appears to be an adz-block was also found (B. 6528). Large chips have been taken from the two faces, and finer chipping at one corner seems to indicate the beginning of shaping. But this may be simply a core, the heart of a piece of rock from which fragments for implements have been struck. The specimen is 3.5 inches long, 1.8 inches in maximum width, and 1.4 inches in maximum thickness.

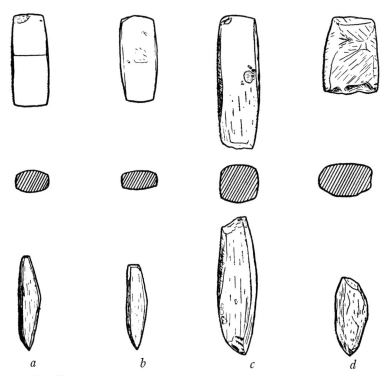

a   b   c   d

FIGURE 65.—Front view, cross section, and profile of adzes and chisel from Bowl Cave, Necker Island: *a, b,* ground adzes; *c,* chisel; *d,* piece of dike rock artificially bevelled on under surface to form a blade.

The rectangular block of basalt shown in figure 63, *b* seems to be an adz-block. The front and back have been split off by a single blow, the ends chipped off by percussion; one side is the original surface of the rock, the other side is ground smooth and convex. Evidently the entire shaping from this point on, was to be by grinding, commencing with the sides.

A cutting tool, presumably a chisel, found with the ground adzes resembles them in every particular except that it is relatively thicker and narrower (fig. 65, *c*). The color is a light blue-gray. The cutting edge and poll have been badly battered.

The angular point of a splinter of dike rock (fig. 63, *c*) from Bowl Cave, has been retouched on one side and partly ground and polished, probably for use as an awl.

TABLE 3.—WEIGHT AND MEASUREMENTS OF ADZES, REJECTS, AND CHISEL FROM BOWL CAVE.

SPECIMEN	WEIGHT OUNCES	MAX. LENGTH INCHES	MAX. THICKNESS INCHES	WIDTH EDGE	L-C INDEX *a*	L-T INDEX *b*	FIGURE
Adz	6	4.25	.8	1.35	31.4	18.5	64, *a*
Adz	3.5	3	.75	1.1	35.5	25.	64, *b*
Adz	3	2.9	.75	1.2	42.4	26.	64, c
Adz	1	1.95	.45	.7	36.	22.	65, *a*
Adz	1	1.85	.45	.6	31.9	23.4	65, *b*
Chisel	2.5	2.85	.75	.6	20.8	26.3	65, c
Adz	1.5	1.7	1.1	1.	......	......	65, *d*
Reject	14.	4.2	1.7	1.7	......	......	....
Reject	2.	2.1	.55	......	......	......	....

[a] L-C index is the width of the edge divided by the length, giving approximately the proportion of breadth to length.
[b] L-T index is the maximum thickness divided by the length, giving the relative thickness.

SINKERS

Two sinkers (fig. 66), having all the characteristics of the Hawaiian squid-lure sinkers, but differing in workmanship, were dug from Bowl Cave. They are of compact basalt heavily patinated. The bottom of the larger is widely and deeply grooved while that of the smaller is not grooved

FIGURE 66.—Drawings showing top, bottom, profile, and cross section of squid-lure sinkers from Bowl Cave, Necker Island: *a*, length 3.3 inches, maximum width 2 inches, maximum height 1.5 inches, weight 10 ounces; *b*, length 3.6 inches, maximum width 2.3 inches, maximum height 1.5 inches, weight 11 ounces.

but is roughly pecked. As viewed from below the ends of both sinkers are squared. Over the top of the sinkers runs a sharp, filed groove. The sides of the sinkers are almost vertical and make a sharp angle with the almost horizontal top.

A small net or line sinker (fig. 67, *b*), also discovered in Bowl Cave, is a rough, flat, vesicular-basalt pebble, encircled by a crudely made longitudinal groove.

a   *b*

FIGURE 67.—Sketches of line or net sinkers: *a*, top view and cross section of limestone sinker from Nihoa, length 1.4 inches, width 1 inch, thickness .6 inch, weight 1 ounce; *b*, top and side view and cross section of basalt sinker from Bowl Cave, Necker, length 1.25 inches, width 1 inch, thickness .6 inch, weight 1 ounce.

BIRD-SNARING PERCH

To my knowledge, the nearest Polynesian equivalent to the remarkable stone artifact (Pl. XV, *E*) which lay partly exposed on the floor of Bowl Cave is the bird-snaring perch of New Zealand described by Best (4, pp. 470-473). Less closely it resembles the foot rest of a digging stick or a stilt. However, agriculture was not a feature of Necker culture, and stilt walking would have been a perilous if not an impossible pastime on the windy, steep island. Besides, the slender horizontal bar would hardly stand so heavy a strain.

In common with the bird-snaring perch of New Zealand, this object has: 1, a horizontal bar; 2, joined to a vertical bar; 3, which projects downwards further than upwards; 4, the horizontal bar is hooked at the end; and 5, the lower part of the vertical bar which is towards the horizontal bar is flattened to rest against some surface. The main differences are: 1, the under surface of the Necker perch is flat, obviously intended to lie against or upon something; 2, the upper part of the vertical bar lacks the hole for the snaring cord. As the birds of Necker perch on rocks, it is conceivable that the artificial perch has been flattened underneath to rest on a flat-top rock; and as the boring of a hole in the narrow, vertical stone bar would have offered difficulties, the snaring cord may have been carried through a cord loop or some such devise at the top.

If this Necker artifact is truly a bird perch, an interpretation which I provisionally accept, it furnishes an example, along with the bowls and idols, of fine work in stone normally performed in wood.

The stone perch is made of vesicular basalt. The vertical bar is 9 inches long and, on the outside, 1.3 inches wide at the middle, tapering to .8 inches at each end. The thickness is 1 inch tapering to .7 inches at each end. The perch projects 4.4 inches.

CONTAINERS

VESSELS

A stone pot was brought back from Necker Island in 1894 by the annexation party. The Tanager Expedition found an unfinished oval bowl on the ridge just east of Bowl Hill and a large, finished oval bowl in Bowl Cave, together with four broken oval bowls and a broken stone jar. All these containers in Bowl Cave lay completely buried in the floor dust except the unbroken bowl, the rim outlining its boat shape, projected two inches above the level floor. One of the broken oval bowls is coated inside and out with soot from the fire of the earth oven. The material of the vessels as determined by Dr. A. S. Palmer is basalt, though altered in appearance through being impregnated with guano. The complete bowl, upon several days test held water perfectly.

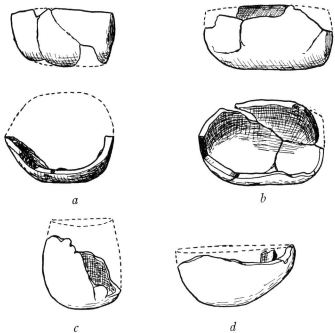

a   *b*

c   *d*

FIGURE 68.—Vessels from Bowl Cave, Necker Island: *a* and *b*, square-end pointed bowls; *c*, jar; *d*, oval bowl.

Jar.—The rounded, thin shell of the bottom and part of the sides of a deep, broad mouthed, subcylindrical bowl, or jar (fig. 68, *c*) is the only vessel of its kind from Necker. Such jars from Nihoa having the same diameter are a little over 8 inches tall.

Pot.—The deep, circular vessel with a flat bottom and diverging sides collected in 1894 I called a pot because of its resemblance to flower pots and because of the need to differentiate it from the round bottom jars (Pl. XVII, *F*). All surfaces are even but the grain of the rock imparts a certain roughness. The rim is flat and .75 inches thick; the bottom is only .25 inches thick. A small rough fragment has broken from it revealing this extreme and fatal thinness.

Oval bowls.—Of the six oval bowls (using oval in its stricter sense) four have one end pointed, the other end squared (Pl. XIX, *E, F*; fig. 68, *a, b*). The remaining two had a rounded broad end and possibly a pointed narrow end (fig. 68, *d*). Their missing forward rim leaves the narrow end in doubt.

The thickness of the walls of the vessels is uniform, the thickness of the bottom is the same or a trifle thicker. The bottoms of the bowls are convex, the sides are slightly convex and vertical in the square-end bowls, though more diverging in the others. The rim is flat. The unfinished bowl (Pl. XIX, *E*) shows that the manufacture was carried on locally and by first roughly shaping the outside. The excavation commenced with a small scoop-shaped cavity.

DISH

Among the containers lying buried in Bowl Cave was the oval dish (Pl. XIX, *B*). It has a squared end and a rounded narrow end.

TABLE 4.—CONTAINERS FROM NECKER ISLAND

(Measurements in inches)

DESCRIPTION	HEIGHT	MAXIMUM LENGTH	MAXIMUM WIDTH	RIM THICKNESS	BOTTOM	WEIGHT POUNDS	ILLUS-TRATION
Jar	?		7.25		.5		fig. 68, *c*
Pot	8		7.8	.75	.25	3.2+	Pl. XVII, *F*
Oval-pointed bowl	7	12.5	10.	1.	1.3	19.	Pl. XIX, *F*
Oval-pointed bowl	4.25	8.25	7. ±			1.2+	fig. 68, *a*
Oval-pointed bowl in rough	8	15.	11.			40.	Pl. XIX, *E*
Oval-pointed bowl	4.25	10.25	8.25	.75	.75	4. +	fig. 68, *b*
Oval bowl	5.	10.25	7.	.5	.5		fig. 68, *d*
Oval dish	2.	9.25	5.25		.25	1.1	Pl. XIX, *b*

MISCELLANEOUS STONE IMPLEMENTS

Most of the beach pebbles excavated from Bowl Cave were brought to the Bishop Museum. They average 2 inches in diameter and 8 inches in height. Thirteen of these are shiny pebbles of very compact basalt, quite unsuited to be heated for the Polynesian oven. Six are porous stones, some of them coated with soot and undoubtedly used for the oven. The smooth pebbles were probably kept for rubbing or throwing stones—only one shows the slightest trace of having been used for hammering. Two small coral pebbles may have been used for rubbing.

Except for the encircling roughly pecked groove, the grooved stone (Pl. XIX, *D*) found by Mr. Edward L. Caum on the slope below Marae 12 appears to be naturally shaped. There are no similar groove-encircled stones in Bishop Museum, but the several naturally round or oval grooved stones suggest sinkers of some sort. The stone from Necker may well have served as a weapon or phallic symbol.

WOOD FRAGMENTS

A partly decayed section of a *wiliwili* (*Erythrina monosperma*) branch or trunk 8 inches long and 3 inches in diameter, and also two much smaller fragments of the same wood were excavated from the floor of Bowl Cave. This, the lightest of all Hawaiian woods, was commonly used for the float of outrigger canoes. It may have drifted to Necker from the larger Hawaiian islands.

Numerous bits of carbonized wood were collected from earth ovens in Bowl Cave.

SKELETAL MATERIAL

The right and left femurs and tibia of a human skeleton were unearthed from the deeper dust of the floor of Bowl Cave among the bowl fragments, adzes, and oven stones. No other bones were discovered, although all the earth of the floor was sifted through a half-inch screen. As the femur and tibia of the right leg are well preserved, and no right fibula or bones of the foot were found, it is certain that the bones do not represent an original interment, but they may represent a reburial. The upper end of the right femur being blackened as if by carbonization has led to the suggestion that the bones are evidences of cannibalism. Against such an assumption is the fact that the best preserved of the bones are not broken for the extraction of marrow and the poorly preserved femur and tibia of the left leg were probably broken by weathering. The long and heavy bones of the leg were most in favor among fishermen for the manufacture of fishhooks and it may be for this purpose that the bones were taken to Bowl Cave.

The right femur is 41.75 cm. long and the right tibia, 34.8 cm. Using the tables of Martin (33), these figures give a reconstructed stature of about 5 feet, 3.5 inches. In spite of its short length, the femur appears to be that of an adult male. The extremities of the left femur have decayed. All that was brought back of the left tibia are the distal extremity and a few fragments of the shaft, all in poor condition.

IMAGES

LOCATION

The Necker images are all male human figures carved in a conventionalized form. Eight are in Bishop Museum collections, two in the British Museum, and three are known through photographs. It is probable that the best of the images which have been taken from Necker are preserved in these two museums. Of the seven images (Pls. XX, *A*; XXI, *A, B, C, D*; XXIII, *C*) brought back from one marae by the Hawaiian annexation party of May 27, 1894, the five finest were obtained for Bishop Museum. In September of the same year, men of the *H. M. S. Champion* landed on Necker and evidently conducted a thorough search for images. How many they succeeded in finding is not known, but two and very likely the finest two, were presented by the officers of the *Champion* to the British Museum (Pl. XXII). Two (Pls. XX, *B* and XXIII, *B*) inferior images were given to the Atkinson family of Honolulu. These last four images had been broken by weathering very much more than the images collected by the annexation party, hence it is my belief that they were formed from the pieces left by that party who had had the pick of the lot (pp. 56-57). The images the annexation party discovered were all at one marae from which they did not have time to gather all the fragments. The only statement which the officers of the *Champion* have left on record concerning the images they collected is that images were found at only one of the maraes (13 a): "On all prominent points overlooking the sea there were platforms . . . on one of these images were found."

The late Dr. William T. Brigham, who went to Necker Island with Minister J. A. King, in July, 1895, failed to find even as much as a missing limb of the first images collected. Undoubtedly they were discouraged in their search by the proof of the *Champion's* visit (p. 58).

As it appears quite certain from Dr. Brigham's luckless search that the *Champion* visitors had gathered all the image fragments left at the one marae where Norton and Freeman discovered the idols, it may be said with confidence that the images collected by the *Champion* were from the same marae. Four images are known to have been collected by the *Champion* and this would seem to be about the number probably left by Norton and Freeman.

Four image specimens found on Necker, two by Gerrit P. Wilder on October 6, 1919, and two after an exhaustive search by the Tanager Expedition in 1923 and 1924, are without much doubt all which have been taken from the island since 1894. Bishop Museum would hardly have failed to learn of other images had they been collected.

None of the four images recently collected was found on a marae. The reshaped, headless and armless figure (Pl. XXIII, *A*) was picked up by Wilder, 100 feet northwest of Marae 1. The reshaped arm (Pl. XIX, *C*) was found by me 100 feet northwest of Marae 12, on the talus slope below it. At the foot of the slope and due west of Marae 12, Wilder picked up the leg which appears to belong with the head (Pl. XXIII, *B*) collected by men of the *Champion*. The texture and color of the basalt of the head and leg agree and the proportion between the two are those characteristic of an image. Furthermore, I have determined that the leg could not possibly belong to any of the other three legless images.

The Tanager Expedition found the heavy, unfinished image (Pl. XXIII, *D-F*) 8.5 feet west and down hill from the southwest corner of Marae 12, where it had evidently been thrown since split by weathering (p. 104). It is natural for it to have been thrown out of Marae 12 as a worthless curio, either by the annexation party or by the *Champion* party. A different story of discovery is Norton's description of finding all the images on one marae and undisturbed by human agency. Without his invaluable account there would be no direct evidence that the stone images were associated with only one of the many maraes.

The location which Captain Norton gives for the marae where the images were discovered is exactly that of Marae 12, in the immediate vicinity of which three image fragments found since the scramble for idols in 1894 were picked up. One of the recently collected fragments is part of one of the *Champion* images presumably collected at the same marae. Captain Norton's description agrees with Marae 12 relative to the partly enclosing wall, the smaller size when compared with the marae on the summit of Annexation Hill, the better appearance, and the impression it produced of a central place of worship. His mention of the lack of uprights would seem to be a serious objection to this identification, were it not that Marae 12 is exceptional in not having uprights standing on a platform; they stand on the terrace and practically against the wall across the front. It would be most natural for one who admittedly was paying little attention to the structure to think of the uprights as part of the wall (Pl. XII, *A*), and to remember only a wall after a lapse of 33 years.

Another fact, which by itself would mean little, tends to confirm my belief that Marae 12 is beyond doubt the place where the images were found. The Tanager Expedition brought back pieces of rough coal from a campfire in front of the fourth upright from the right of Marae 12. Norton said the expedition with which he was associated took no food ashore and made no fire. Men of the British gunboat *Champion* are the only people whom there is reason to suppose had previously stayed some time or overnight on the island—the *Champion,* of course, burned coal. If, as Norton says, many idol fragments were left on the marae where they were discovered, then the British men would have spent some time there and may well have made a camp.

As it is fairly certain the Necker stone images were made on the island (p. 118), and came from one marae, where are the images of the 32 other maraes? Supposing each were furnished with an average of 6 images, instead of the 11 of the one marae on Flagpole Hill, there would then be more than 200. The work of producing this number of images on the island should have left more traces than one hammerstone and one idol in the rough. The most natural assumption is that, if other images existed, they were not manufactured on the island, and that if made elsewhere they were of perishable wood. It would seem that even if the images had been brought to the island and then carried away, they were of wood, else some of them would have survived on the neighboring islands.

DESCRIPTION OF IMAGES

The Necker images are composed of vesicular basalt, varying in color from light to dark gray. Though the shaping has been done primarily by pecking, there is evidence also of considerable filing or rubbing. The grooves between the legs are of a smoothness such as would result from grinding. In the unfinished image (Pl. XXIII, *D-F*) the legs have been shaped, the arms blocked out, the chin of the head outlined. The head had therefore been left to the last as in Marquesan workmanship, as described by Linton (32, p. 71).

The statuettes range from 8 to 18 inches high, and weigh from 4 to 25 pounds, inclining equally to these two extremes. The remarkable sameness of the images is ample proof that rigid conventionalization had settled on the minds of the Necker people. Certainly, if they could have carved out of the rough, hard basalt of Necker one after another image of such symmetry, sharpness, and evenness of every part, they could have achieved a more naturalistic figure had they the idea in mind. The images vary most in the shape of the legs, but this is more a degree of finish than a fundamental difference.

The head is more than a fourth the height of the body, and in some more than a third. It is without a neck and sets so low on the shoulders that the base of the nose is on or below the level of them. The ears consequently are at or very close to the juncture of the head with the shoulders. The full chin comes well down on the chest. The large, rounded ears stand out at right angles to the head. In front they are concave, in back convex. The back of the head is rounded and, in some, curves inwards towards the shoulders. The forehead slopes steeply back to the top of the head. The brow ridges on most of the images are naturalistic, appearing in delicate relief on the forehead—a surprising detail in view of the usual grotesque treatment of the parts. The brow ridges merge in the base of the nose. The nose is straight, and, in four figures slopes outward toward the base, remaining practically the same width from root to base. The eyes are square or slightly rounded knobs in the same relief as the nose. The mouth is very wide, the lips represented as parted and the tongue protruding. The upper and lower lips are in equal relief, the upper lip horizontal, the lower curved downward. The tongue, in higher relief, extends from one corner of the mouth to the other. The chin and lower part of the face is raised on the chest. In two images (Pl. XXI, *C, D*) the chin is considerably thrust out and is rounded underneath.

The trunk is slab-like, the sides meet the front and back at a sharp angle. The sides curve inward to a marked degree in the smaller figures. The front and back are flat or slightly convex, transversely. Longitudinally the front is vertical or sloping outward at a small angle towards the base. There is no modelled belly and no representation of a navel. The back slopes slightly outward to the buttocks, which in most specimens are indicated by a swelling. On at least five images the buttocks are divided by a sharp groove part way up the back. The male sex is indicated by a rounded, horizontally projecting knob at the base of which are two pendant lobes in relief.

The arms hang down straight from the shoulder and are of the same length as the trunk. Hands and fingers are not indicated. The arms were separated from the body by the cutting of a V-shaped groove an equal distance in from the front and from the back. A sharp ridge is left in a median line on the sides of the trunk and on the inner sides of the arms. The ridge marks the meeting of the front and back grooves. The arms of image, shown in Plate XXI, *C,* are unusual in having the lower part reduced on the outside.

The legs are quite short and heavy on all except three images (Pls. XXI, *C, D* and XXII, *A*) which have more natural proportions. The legs are completely separated by a narrow groove which has been cut in from the front and back like the arms, but the median ridge has been removed in all but one specimen (Pl. XXI, *B*). The lower leg tapers from the knee which is indicated in the three most finished figures by a restriction in the size of the leg, and in others by a meeting of the plane of the thigh with the inbending plane of the lower part of the leg. Two images have feet (Pls. XXI, *C*;

XXII,*A*) with heels but not toes. A fret along the front of the legs of image shown in Plate XXI, *A* would seem to represent an abbreviated foot.

The carving (Pl. XXIII, *A*) has the legs of a Necker image of the smallest dimensions. The upper part, however, is simply a rounded projection. That arms were once on the carving is certain from the presence of the median ridge on the sides of the trunk. This ridge has been left on all the images after the space between the arms and the trunk was cut through. If originally there had been a face, it was completely obliterated in reshaping when the sides from which the arms sprung were reduced to a smooth, rounded surface. It should be noted that the male sexual organs are not present. Perhaps the whole carving has been reshaped to represent them. The upper part of some Polynesian images of human form as shown by Handy (21, p. 121) and by Stokes (44) plainly represent an upright penis.

The image shown in Plate XXIII, *D-F,* resembles a figure which has lost a head resting on a neck. However, the heads of Necker images are neckless and rest mainly on the chest, and a careful examination shows that the head of this figure is no exception. What appears to be the lower margin of the breast is really that of the chin upon which work had commenced. The face has been roughly pecked flat, the smooth part of the upper right side being the original waterworn surface of beach stone. The top of the head is extensively scarred. A large piece of material has became dislodged in the position of the image's left shoulder, on the back. This occurred subsequently to the shaping on the back because the broken surface encroaches upon finished work. Perhaps the dislodgment was caused by a faulty blow in shaping the shoulder thus accounting for the stopping of the work. At any rate, it would seem to have occurred at the time in which the figure was made as the damaged surface is fully as much weathered as the contiguous surfaces, whereas the broken surfaces of the leg are clearly much fresher, although the break is typical of the weather splitting of the other images and shows as much subsequent weathering as some. However, the image as it was found on the slope below Marae 12, face down, 8.5 feet west of the southwest corner, had been disturbed by human hands since the splitting of the leg, because the leg was at least 3 feet away among rocks, where it could hardly have been rolled by birds. I believe this disturbance took place in the search for idols in 1894.

PIECE OF SCULPTURING

On the talus slope below and 100 feet to the northwest of Marae 12, I picked up what appeared to be the right arm of a Necker image (Pl. XIX, *C*). It lay on the surface of the slope, conspicuous because of its smoothness and because of its lighter color in comparison with the surrounding stones. A search of the slope failed to reveal any other shaped pieces.

The arms of all known Necker Island images are marked with a sharp ridge on the inner side and a horizontal extremity or one that slopes up outwardly. There is no trace of an inner ridge on this piece and the well finished extremity slopes up inwardly. If this piece is an arm then, surely, it belongs to a type of figure differing from the others, unless it has been reshaped, as has the headless and armless figure (Pl. XXIII, *A*). It is my belief that both of these have been reshaped into phallic form. To suppose the specimen which seems to have been an arm was originally a penis of a statue, presupposes an image of immense size whereas the Necker images found on the same slope, are all less than 18 inches long, and the average size of their arms is about the size of the reshaped piece. Since the images first seen were not broken or thrown about by human hands, it is not likely a great image was carelessly removed by the Necker people or that foreign visitors have removed a great image without leaving record.

The piece which seems to be a naturalistic representation of a penis is 6 inches long and slightly curved. It is oval in cross section, the point of the oval turned to the inner side of the curve. The maximum diameter at the base is 1.9 inches; at the other end, 1.65 inches. It is smoothly pecked all over except where the break occurred. The material is gray, rather compact basalt.

COMPARISONS

RELIGIOUS STRUCTURES

A few structures on Nihoa are very similar if not identical with the Necker maraes. Those exhibiting most clearly the relationship are the two adjoining maraes, Site 50. The arrangement of their uprights essentially follows the plan of those of the Necker marae; that is, a row of an odd number of rear uprights with a specialized central upright, and single uprights and pairs of uprights arranged medially and laterally.

The rear uprights of the upper marae, Site 50, Nihoa, are set on the floor of the terrace instead of on a platform as also are the rear uprights of five varying Necker maraes (p. 67). The pair of central rear uprights of the Nihoa marae, with the slab tilting outward before them, are comparable to the pair of waterworn, central rear uprights of the variant Marae 12 on Necker, which has a pair of tilting slabs before them. (Compare Pl. VII, *B* and Pl. XII, *A*.) The central and right uprights of this Nihoa marae have many parallels on Necker, and the left uprights, while not duplicated at any one Necker marae, have all the three positions covered by uprights of Maraes 18, 21, and 32. Most of the uprights on the Nihoa marae are slabs, but four of them are dike prisms. Dike prism uprights are exceedingly rare on Necker, but they do appear (Marae 21 and the varying Maraes 11 and 18).

The lower marae, Site 50, rises in three steps instead of two, the maximum number in Necker maraes. The middle step is probably simply a devise to extend the terrace without the necessity of elevating the front another foot and a half, rather than a ceremonial prerequisite. Omitting the middle step, the arrangement of uprights is in every respect parallel to arrangements of uprights on the ordinary Necker marae. The side walls of this Nihoa marae are comparable to the side walls of the variant Marae 9 on Necker.

The affinity of the two Nihoa maraes, Site 50, is thus seen to be rather with the several partly enclosed, platformless Necker maraes than with its ordinary, unenclosed platform maraes. The uprights of all except for minor variations, are nearly identical in arrangement. The one Necker marae, the tiny Marae 11, which seems not to fit in with the others except in having uprights orderly arranged, bears some resemblance to the much larger Nihoa ruin at Site 10.

In both a low, ill defined wall runs along the front and encloses each end of a terrace on the edge of the bluff of the bay, and a pair of uprights stand parallel to the front retaining wall. (Compare fig. 31 and Pl. I, *B*.)

A dike prism lies on the terrace floor, Site 11, Necker; a large number of dike prisms lie on a corner of the wall at the Site 10, Nihoa. The Nihoa ruin does not have two right uprights and it does have coral heads deposited on its outer corners, differing in these respects from the Necker marae. To my mind, the coral heads of the Nihoa ruin make of it a fishermen's shrine, but this use may be subsequent. However, if the entire structure was set up by the ritualists employing coral heads as offerings, then the Necker Marae 11, though not having coral upon it, may also have been a fishermen's shrine. At Nuu, Maui, I have seen a fishermen's shrine (*koa*) which was a terrace on the bluff of the bay, enclosed on the front and sides by a low wall, but there were no uprights or coral heads.[6]

Stokes (45, p. 19) has recorded two upright stones connected with, though not on, a *koa* at Pearl Harbor, Oahu. One is a dark stone, 4.5 feet high, representing Kuula, a patron of fishermen, the other a coral stone slab 2.5 feet high, representing his wife, Hina.

I noted at Kahue, Lanai, a pair of basalt uprights 3 feet high standing at an outside corner of a *koa* (17, p. 70). Neither Stokes nor I have seen uprights on a Hawaiian *koa* or remember seeing dike stones laid upon them.

The small, rough, coral strewn platform which is the commonest form of Hawaiian *koa* (*ko'a*), is duplicated on Nihoa by structures at Sites 6, 9, and 11. It has no parallel on Necker, unless it be in the three small, bare, irregular pavements, Sites L, M, and N, on the eastern extremity of the island.

The Nihoa terraces with rows of dike prism uprights extending across them do not exist on Necker, but the unique group of seven waterworn uprights at the southwest corner of Marae 20, Necker, suggests the same idea. Comparable with this Necker marae is the large terrace, Site 51, Nihoa. It also has seven uprights (dike prisms) at the same end, a pair of slab uprights standing in the middle and facing the slab uprights at the opposite end. However, the corresponding end of this Nihoa structure is now occupied by a Hawaiian type of *koa,* and because the two uprights appear to have no connection with the *koa* I believe they are the remnant of a row of rear uprights which, if all present, would show the structure to be a marae similar to the Necker Marae 20.

The group of slender uprights at Marae 20, Necker, and Site 51, Nihoa, when compared with each other and then with the group of uprights of similar size and spacing on the Nihoa terraces, Sites 28, 40, 41, and 45, reveal a close physical relationship, the significance of which is puzzling. It

---

[6] In a crevice of the bluff rising over this *koa* was found in 1922 a stone fetish wrapped in a Hawaiian newspaper dated 1916, beside it was a piece of dried awa root. It was learned from an eye witness that a temporary house just large enough for the kahuna to crawl into was erected on the *koa* when his revelation dream was required. In a corner was an umu where the sacrificial pig was baked.

looks almost as if this feature of a group of slender uprights, arranged more or less in rows, grew up with the Necker marae and then became independent of it, or even perhaps supplemented it. It surely was in use on Nihoa until the very last habitation because one of these arrangements of the prisms at Site 41, Nihoa, was imposed on a dwelling site which had been occupied by natives familiar with the historic Hawaiian culture.

Elsewhere in Hawaii, platforms or terraces with arrangements of stone uprights, such as are found on Nihoa and Necker, have not been discovered nor are they mentioned in early descriptions. However, Webber (9, pl. 33) illustrates a rectangular enclosed heiau on Kauai, which has a dike prism upright about the middle. The upright is wrapped with a tapa scarf. At one end of the walled enclosure is a long, low, and narrow platform with upright wooden slabs along the back. Before the platform stands a single wooden slab and further out on the floor of the heiau, a pair of wooden slabs. The slabs seem to be 3 to 5 feet high and have a human face carved on them (Pl. XIV). I have no doubt that the carved slab found in opening an irrigation ditch on Kauai in 1896, and now in the Bishop Museum (No. 8049) is one of the slabs such as the artist Webber was depicting. The disposition of the wooden slabs on the Kauai heiau seems to be fundamentally that of the stone uprights of the Necker marae and the logical assumption is that the wooden slabs were the surviving equivalent of them, the front central upright, a dike prism, alone retaining the original form and material. If wooden slabs were used on the heiaus of the Hawaiian temple, then the mystery of the absence on heiau ruins of uprights, such as are found on Nihoa and Necker, is partly cleared. However, the illustration made by Arago (1, pl. 87) and the one by Ellis (14, p. 181) of heiaus on the island of Hawaii, showing the same end as the Kauai heiau, reveal no slabs of any kind. The rear images are carved in the round and arranged in a semicircle.

The plan of the Kauai heiau illustrated in Cook's atlas certainly is not universal on Kauai. This statement is based on my observation of two heiaus on Kauai, that at Kee, Haena, and at Apahukalea, Wainiha, and from the 7 plans of other Kauai heiaus, made by Thrum (48, pp. 52-67). Of 39 heiaus on the island of Hawaii, of which plans are on file in Bishop Museum only one, the heiau of Haleaama at Holualoa, Kona, has uprights. These, however, are three slabs set on edge in a row across the middle of a simple platform and parallel to the small ends. The possibility is thus apparent that the use of slabs was not only restricted to Kauai but to certain of the Kauai heiaus. To be sure, a row of 9 upright stones placed a few inches apart, has been observed on Lanai (17, p. 72, pl. 5, *b*), but as these were set on a limited level area between constantly shifting sand dunes, I believe they had been placed there quite recently. Nothing like them was seen elsewhere on Lanai, so the structure is too uncertain to be taken seriously.

A wide difference of plan exists between the ruins of Hawaiian heiaus and Necker maraes: whereas the plans of many Hawaiian heiaus are intricate and all of them exhibit the greatest diversity among themselves, no two being alike in proportions or arrangements, the Necker maraes are simple and exhibit a marked uniformity. From the work of Linton (32) it appears that the Hawaiian heterogeniety of temple plans is equalled in the Marquesas, but my observations show that in the Society Islands each of three or four related types is uniform through all its representatives. One of these Society Island types has its distribution sharply limited to the interior of Tahiti and Moorea, where it is the only form of marae known (16). It is characterized by a low narrow platform at one end of a rectangular, open court. Along the rear of the platform are an uneven number of stone slab uprights, the middle upright being the larger. Against the middle front of the platform is another slab upright, and in line with this and the rear central upright, and further out from the platform is a single dike prism upright or a pair of prism uprights. There are also uprights on the right and left borders of the court. Obviously the maraes of interior Tahiti and Moorea are more closely related to the Necker maraes than are the Hawaiian heiaus.

A few of the smaller Tahitian inland maraes have their rear row of uprights planted directly in the court floor as in the five varying maraes on Necker. At Ieiefaatau, in the depths of Papenoo Valley, Tahiti, and a few yards from an ordinary marae, is a small rectangular enclosure with three rows of stone uprights, some of them slabs, others dike prisms, stretched across it. Several odd uprights stand off to the sides of the rows. This is the arrangement of the puzzling rows of uprights on several Nihoa terraces, in particular Sites 40 and 41. I cite these parallels now, because they establish the religious character of the Nihoa-Necker structures with uprights, and at the same time force the conclusion that these Nihoa-Necker erections are basic Polynesian religious structures and not some local and unimportant freak development. The demonstration of the precise relationship between Tahitian and Necker-Nihoa maraes will have to await the publication of the detailed description of the Tahitian ruins.

Close as is the similarity between the inland Tahitian maraes and the Necker maraes, those of the northwest Tuamotu archipelago seem equally close. Seurat (40, pp. 475-484) gives detailed descriptions and illustrations of several of them. A low, narrow platform faces on an open court. Upright stone slabs are set along the rear of the platform. Two maraes are described each with three rear uprights (fig. 69). Out on the court, in line with one of the central rear uprights, stands a slab on end, facing on a tiny platform suggestive of the flat slab placed before a number of corresponding uprights on Necker.   The illustration of the marae of Katipa (fig. 63) at Fakahina Island, shows a tiny platform placed against the main platform and in line with a rear upright.   This feature appears to be represented on

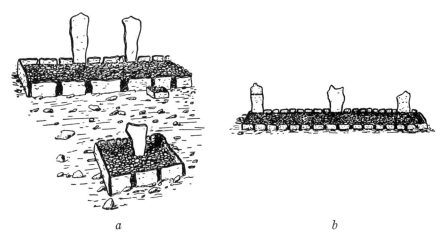

a   b

FIGURE 69.—Sketches of maraes in the Tuamotu archipelago: *a*, one end of the Marae Katipa, Fakahina Island, showing the sacred stone uprights, a small altar before one of the uprights, and a small platform supporting an upright; *b*, Marae Ramapohia, Fagatau Island, Tuamotu archipelago, platform about 3 feet wide, 60 feet long, the upright slabs of limestone about 6 feet high, the carving on left slab representing the human form is called *ofai tiki* or representation of a deity.
(Reproduced by permission from a drawing by Seurat.)

Necker by the tiny platform placed in the same manner before the rear central upright of Sites 1, 6, 14, 21, 22, and 31.   Seurat learned that this little platform of the Tuamotu marae served for the kneeling place of the priest. The rear uprights represented divinities.   Some of the rear uprights were cut in rude human form: a projection at the top representing the head and a flange on each side, the arms.

Seurat remarks that on the island of Fakahina the maraes were numerous (he mentions 16 by name) and that each family seems to have had its own.

Best (4, p. 289) states that in New Zealand, some of the places where rites were performed by native priests were marked by a row of upright, unworked, stone slabs set directly in the ground.   If Samoa or Tonga have systems of uprights connected with their places of worship, they remain to be described.

Concerning the nature of the Nihoa-Necker maraes and the function of their uprights there is hope that considerable may be learned when all the material available covering the use of the analogous Tuamotu, New Zealand, and Tahitian structures has been carefully studied. Henry (26, pp. 134-35) mentions memorial stones placed along the front of the platform, stone up-rights out on the court marking the position where those who had an interest in the marae leaned or knelt during marae ceremonies, and a row of stone uprights which held "small figures of men made of coconut braided leaves, representing in effigy the priests praying. . . ." at the end of the court op-posite the platform which was called the *ahu*. Wilson (51, p. 208) was given a demonstration of the use of an upright stone placed a few paces before the marae platform. The native "went a few yards back [before the platform], and laying hold of an upright stone, like a grave-stone, he knelt with one knee, and looking upwards, began to call on the Eatooa [*atua*], by crying, 'Whooo, whooo,' and by afterwards making a whistling noise, intimated it to be the way in which the Eatooa answered them."

IMAGES

For comparison with the Necker images no examples of sculpture have been found on Nihoa. Few genuine Hawaiian stone human figures are known and these are the roughest crudities, lacking in uniformity. The body is slightly shaped, the limbs barely indicated if at all. The arms, when shown, rest on the abdomen. Sex is not indicated. The neckless head is upturned, the mouth is opened but there is no protruding tongue. Not only are the stone images quite different from those of Necker, but, as is obvious, they were very rarely made. Although the Hawaiian wooden images are carefully and entirely formed, there is none in collections which is like the Necker images. The Hawaiian images have a neck, naturalistic eyes, a nose wide at the base, and variously distorted mouths. The temple images are grotesque and conventional in the extreme and carved in one piece with a long pedestal. The more naturalistic portable household human images which are about the same sizes as the Necker figures and also without a pedestal, are closer in appearance to them.

About all that Hawaiian and Necker images have in common are most of the generic characters of the human figures of the rest of marginal Poly-nesia, excepting Easter Island. Such are the exaggeratedly large head carved with more completeness to detail than the rest of the body, widely stretched mouth and protruding tongue, a standing position with flexed knees and heavy lower legs. Although the treatment of the arms of Necker images is exclusively Hawaiian—the arms hanging straight down their full length—the treatment of the head and body, far more than any other images in Polynesia, is akin to the Marquesan stone statues and statuettes. As described by Linton (31, p. 181; 32, p. 70) these are replicas of the more numerous wooden ones and served in the same capacities. In both places the human figure is entirely formed and skillfully carved in planes which meet in sharply defined angles. The face is remarkably flat, a wide chin rests low on the chest, the mouth is widely stretched with parallel lips and tongue in relief, the ears are flange-like, the eyebrows are in delicate relief merging in the base of the nose. These traits are not so represented in the Hawaiian images, at least not in combination.

Because of the convention of eyes and nostrils and the arm position, which stamp every well carved Marquesan figure, the connection between the Marquesan and Necker images seems to be more remote than is probably true. The similarity could hardly be expected to be exact, for the comparison is between images of the historic period, conforming to the last development in wood of the typical Marquesan conventions, and images made before the historic period—so long ago that weathering has broken all of them though the material is hard basalt. In this light the comparatively strong similarities which exist indicate that the Necker images were like the Marquesan images before they took on the familiar convention. It is interesting to note that the inscribed stone idol in the Kalasasaya palace, Peru, as illustrated by Posnansky (39, frontispiece) has as many points in common with the Necker images as have the Marquesan. Although the mouth, in being tongueless and proportionately narrow (the lips are parallel and in relief), is not so much like the mouth of the Necker figures as is the Marquesan, the square eyes in relief and the straight nose in the same relief are identical with the Necker eyes and noses.

ADZES

Of three Nihoa adzes, one (fig. 19, *c*) matches every feature of the Necker ground adzes save that the transverse convexity of the front is not so great, a difference well within the range of likely individual variation. Therefore, I believe the adz demonstrates a culture touching both islands. While the other two Nihoa adzes differ from the Necker adzes in having straight sides which converge towards the poll, partial grinding (on the larger adz), and perfectly straight cutting edges, they are undistinguishable from the typical small Hawaiian adz. While the adzes from Necker Island are more closely related to those from other Hawaiian islands than to those of any other area, they show absolute differences: Hawaiian adzes are not, as are the adzes of Necker, wider in the middle than at the cutting edge and poll; few Hawaiian adzes, and those less than 2 inches long, are ground smooth over all surfaces; the surfaces of Hawaiian adzes are not as convex as the Necker adzes, but are ground flat or almost flat; in nearly all Hawaiian adzes the cutting edge is straight as viewed from above and the convexity where present is not so great as in the Necker adzes; no double-bitted adz has come to light from the main Hawaiian group to compare with the Necker adz shown in figure 64, *a*.

Close similarity between Hawaiian and two Nihoa finished adzes may be seen by comparing figure 19, *a, b* with figure 19, *d*.

Is the Necker type of adz to be found in the other Hawaiian islands? In carefully examining 680 Hawaiian adzes, I found only 2 which might be considered of the Necker type; one from Kauai (fig. 19, *e*), the other from Waimea, Oahu (fig. 19, *f*). The length of the first is 3.1 inches, the width of cutting edge .85 inches, the thickness .5 inches; the Oahu adz is 3.5 inches in length, the width of the cutting edge is 1.5 inches, the thickness is .7 inches. Both adzes are widest at the juncture of tang and blade, and are entirely ground smooth though greater than 2 inches in length. The two adzes are relatively of the same thickness as the Necker adzes. The Oahu adz is relatively of the same width, but the Kauai adz is 4 per cent narrower than the narrowest Necker adz (but 6.6 per cent wider than the chisel). However, these two adzes, like the adz of Necker type from Nihoa, have not the convexity of the Necker adzes. Their cutting edges have not the Necker curve but are absolutely straight, a feature which might have been produced by regrinding in later days. I regard these two adzes as of the Necker type and therefore as indicating the former presence of Necker culture in the Hawaiian group.

CONTAINERS

The pot (Pl. XVII, *F*) brought from Necker Island in 1894, remained the solitary example of its kind in the Bishop Museum until 1923, when the Tanager Expedition added a similar stone pot (Pl. XVII, *E*) from Nihoa. The vessel from Necker is of guano impregnated basalt, of which all the Necker Island containers are made. The pot from Nihoa Island in common with all other Nihoa containers, is of locally available firm, vesicular basalt, a rock present on Necker and used in making the images, but not employed in the manufacture of the containers. It seems reasonable to suppose, therefore, that the Nihoa pot was made locally, especially as it is unfinished and differs a little in style, having an almost flat base. In any event, the Necker pot is a product of people who camped on Necker, and the Nihoa pot was either carried to Nihoa from Necker, or what is much more probable, made on Nihoa by people of the same culture.

Obviously the jars were made on both islands by the same people, because the one Necker jar, in what remains of it (fig. 68, *c*) is identical with the jars made on Nihoa save in this significant respect: it is of local material, of which all Necker containers are made.

The two islands had pots and jars in common, but oval bowls have been found only on Necker. This distinction is not as great as it might seem because the oval, pointed dish is represented on both islands and it is but a step from the dish to the bowl of the same shape. Also, the odd, beautifully shaped, rectangular Nihoa shallow bowl (Pl. XVIII, *E*) which has both ends squared, is a likely reflection of the culture which squared one end of the Necker boat-shaped bowls. The form of every Necker container, then, is traceable to Nihoa. The converse is not true. Nihoa has in addition sub-spherical and elliptical bowls made from beach stones and retaining much of the original surface of the stone on their exterior. The workmanship of these small, simple rounded bowls is the crudest, the large elliptical bowls are much more skillfully done, but the height of excellence is attained in the jars. Does not this indicate the development of the Nihoa-Necker fine vessels on the island of Nihoa? They are not found on other Hawaiian islands nor elsewhere in Polynesia, which is not astonishing in view of the unsuitability of stone for the shaping of deep, thin-shell vessels. To smooth the outside and to wear down the great cavity must have been a work of infinite patience and much skill, and the result was a heavy, extremely fragile vessel. Only in the face of the lack of wood and gourds and of a vital need (storage of water) for deep containers would such tasks be undertaken. The natives certainly were confronted with a lack of suitable materials. The parts of gourds found on Nihoa suggest that the gourd plants *Cucurbita maxima* and *Lagenaria vulgaris* may have been introduced and cultivated on Nihoa. However, any people able to reach the islands are unlikely to have made the stone vessels at a period when they possessed gourds.

The Hawaiian stone containers are shallow thick-walled cups, or sub-spherical and cylindrical thick-walled mortars and lamps. One finely ground Hawaiian cup-mortar (Pl. XV, *F*) was unearthed on Nihoa (Site 41), but aside from this, the vessels from Nihoa and Necker are thin-walled and obviously food or water vessels. In form, the stone jars closely resemble the deep Hawaiian wooden bowls (fig. 22, *c*) and the deep gourd vessels of Polynesia in general. While the Nihoa subcylindrical bowls are in form like the common bowls of Hawaii, the large elliptical bowls are restricted to Nihoa. I look upon the elliptical bowls as a local development due to the fact that most large beach stones are elliptical rather than perfectly round.

The pot from Necker and Nihoa, the shallow, rectangular bowl from Nihoa, and the oval bowls from Necker have no parallels in Hawaii. The pot and rectangular bowl may be imitations of wooden bowls which have gone out of use in Hawaii. The classic example of the imitation of a wood bowl in stone is the oval, stone bowl with legs, from the Society Islands, now at Madrid, illustrated by Corney (10, p. xxxvi). However, this was a show piece presented to the king of Tahiti. The boat-shaped bowl may be a specialization from the oval Hawaiian-Nihoa-Necker dish, to be shoved into a niche to collect and store dripping water. That the collecting and storing of water was the function of these bowls, I think there is no room for doubt. There is also the possibility that the boat-shaped bowl is a development from the oval pouring bowl typical of Tahiti and its vicinity, rather than from the oval dish which in gourd appears widely in Polynesia.

The Necker containers are well represented in Nihoa culture. Nihoa has cruder, simpler vessels and a larger number of the finely finished ones, from which I infer that it was the center of the development of these stone containers reported from nowhere else in Polynesia. A characteristic Hawaiian cup mortar which lay buried on Nihoa close to a typical Hawaiian adz refers to the period when Nihoa was connected with the historic culture of Hawaii. The stone vessels of Necker do not belong to the historic Hawaiian culture, as Necker is unknown to its tradition and unrepresented in the culture typical of it. Hence, the stone containers of Nihoa which are like the Necker containers and probably all of the stone vessels from Nihoa belong to a period preceeding the historic Hawaiian. They also point to a time when Nihoa and Necker were not in communication with a land abounding in timber and gourds. The form of their stone vessels indicates previous familiarity with legless, deep, circular and oval Polynesian wooden bowls and gourds.

The jars strongly suggest the deep wooden bowls of Hawaii, but the boat-shaped Necker bowls suggest the oval pouring bowls of the Society Islands. There are fewer points in common between the containers from the Society Islands and the stone containers from Necker and Nihoa than between the stone containers and the Hawaiian wooden containers. Hence, any contribution from the Society Islands should be considered as coming by way of the Hawaiian islands.

SQUID-LURES AND SQUID HOOK SINKERS

The two squid-lure and hook sinkers of Necker are distinguished from the common Hawaiian sinkers by their squared ends and the sharp angle which the sides make with the top. One end of some Hawaiian sinkers is squared, but none of approximately 350 sinkers examined has both ends squared or a quadrangular cross section. Judging from the Necker sinkers, boat-shaped bowls, bird-snaring perch, and idols, angularity appears to be the stamp or Necker workmanship, in this respect, except for adzes, contrasting strongly with the typical Hawaiian.

While squid-hook sinkers have not come to light on Nihoa, the accompanying cowrie lures, absent on Necker, were discovered on Nihoa. Most of these shells are prepared exactly like those from other Hawaiian islands, but a third of them differ in having only one bored hole, that in the larger end.

One of the Nihoa lures (fig. 23) has a piece of cord tied to the larger end and another piece tied to the smaller end. As described by Beasley (5, p. 100) the Hawaiian lures have the suspension line pass through both holes except when two shells are attached to one hook. Then a separate cord is tied to each end of both shells and the suspension cord is attached to the hook. The Nihoa lure was probably mounted in this way. It is also possible that it was fastened in a different way or that it was unmounted and simply tied in a string of shell lures.

The cord in the Nihoa squid lures is made from fibers of the hala (*Pandanus*) root while the cordage of all the mounted Hawaiian lures in the Bishop Museum is of olona (*Touchardia*) twine. Cord brought to Nihoa from Hawaii would probably have been olona, coconut, or hau (*Hibiscus*) fiber. There is no record of hala root fiber being used in any of the islands of Hawaii except Kauai, where present inhabitants—both white and native— remember that it was used extensively especially for house lashings but not for fishing tackle. Hence it is almost safe to assume that the Nihoa cord was introduced from Kauai, or was manufactured locally during a period of cultivation when hala grew and the coconut (and perhaps hau) did not grow on the island. (Olona could not have lived on such a small dry island). Stokes tells me that braid from hala root fibers is extensively used in the Tuamotus. Braid, of one material or another, is used for the suspension lines of squid lures in Central and Southeastern Polynesia.

THE POSITION OF NIHOA AND NECKER CULTURE

The uniformity of the cultural remains on Necker Island is so striking as to leave no doubt that the island was occupied during a single period. That the occupation was not merely an occasion such as the sojourn of a fleet of canoes, is apparent from the large number of maraes and the evidence that all were not built simultaneously.

The Necker maraes outnumber all possible dwelling sites, two to one. As the type of these maraes is that of family and tribally owned maraes in southeast Polynesia, they surely represent a far larger number of people than the island could have supported. It is very doubtful if Necker Island ever completely sustained more than the handful of people who dwelt for a time in Bowl Cave.

Where, then, did the people live who visited Necker for the purpose of erecting maraes or performing rites upon them?

As many as 150 people could have and may have lived on Nihoa, the nearest inhabitable island, where two maraes of the Necker type have been found, yet, the 32 or 33 maraes of Necker are indicative of a much larger population. Assuming, nevertheless, that the Necker people came from Nihoa, the question of their origin still remains to be answered. Accepting the conclusion of Gregory (18a, p. 222) that the islands of Polynesia have not materially altered since man is first likely to have appeared in the Pacific, it seems incredible to suppose the Necker pilgrims came from anywhere outside of the Hawaiian islands.

Nevertheless, the concentration of many religious structures in one place is a phenomenon observed nowhere among the inhabited Hawaiian islands, nor have the Necker maraes been found among them, but such grouping, surprisingly enough, is normal in the Society Islands. I have seen at one spot in the interior of Punaruu Valley, Tahiti, eleven maraes, and these happened to be in many essential features identical with the Necker Island marae.

An analysis of the cultural relationships of the other remains fortunately preserved by Necker's remoteness and inaccessibility, reveal, however, a definite connection between Necker culture and distinctly Hawaiian culture, and lead to the conclusion that the elements of Necker culture lacking in the Hawaiian were formerly present.

No single class of material is quite so helpful as the adz for pointing out probable cultural relationships within Polynesia. This is due to the fact that large series of adzes are available for study from all the larger and many of the smaller Polynesian islands, and to the individuality of Polynesian adzes and the remarkable tenacity and uniformity of each type once evolved or borrowed. So it is that the Necker adzes, with a tang at an angle to the blade exclude central Polynesia (Samoa, Tonga, Niue) from the likely immediate sphere of influence but include marginal Polynesia (Hawaii, Marquesas, Society Islands, New Zealand) where alone in the Pacific this type of adz has been collected. The particular Necker variety of the adz is definitely limited to Hawaii, and yet, among Hawaiian adzes it is quite rare. The class to which the Necker adzes belong is seen to be, from its distribution, a creation of marginal Polynesia, and in the presence of logical prototypes in the Marquesas and Tahiti, but not in Hawaii, to have been evolved in and introduced from the southeast.

The thin-shell stone vessels and the T-shaped bird-snaring perch from Bowl Cave are objects which elsewhere in Polynesia were made of wood, and which are unsuited to be fashioned of unyielding, heavy, brittle stone. Consequently they bear testimony to a time when the people inhabiting Bowl Cave were cut off from communication with timber-bearing land and thereby forced to manufacture whatever objects of large diameter they required out of stone or drift wood. The same pinch of environment must have prevailed when the images for Marae 12 were made. The marked sharpness of all features and the careful separation of arms from the body are a style of carving for the realization of which wood offers the least difficulties and basalt the most. Furthermore this peculiar angular, sharply-defined style is that of the implements and utensils in Bowl Cave, making it highly probable that its occupants were the carvers of the images and the owners of Marae 12 where the images were found. At least, it can not be doubted that the objects in Bowl Cave belong to the same cultural strata as the images and the marae, and therefore can be taken as representatives of the culture of the marae builders.

The stone vessels, bird-snaring perch, and images of Necker are not found in the main Hawaiian islands nor in other parts of Polynesia, which fact, together with the unfinished Necker bowl and image, confirms the supposition that they were made on Necker, and except for the vessels on Nihoa, on Necker only. The Necker-Nihoa jars and dish have wooden equivalents in Hawaii; the oval-pointed bowls of Necker, in southeast Polynesia. The pot is confined to Nihoa and Necker. Comparing wooden bowls of today with stone copies of wooden bowls made long ago, and not finding wooden equivalents of all the stone bowls gives solid ground for believing that these forms of wooden bowls ceased to be manufactured during the historic period. This is also true of such human figures as the Necker images, which are not anywhere now represented in wood. Their arm position is that of Hawaiian figures but opposed to that of the rest of marginal Polynesia, but otherwise the Necker figures have most in common with the Marquesan. This is explainable if the Necker images are regarded as embodying the features of a marginal Polynesian prototype.

It should be noted that no stone human images are recorded from central Polynesia or Micronesia, and extremely few from Melanesia. The Polynesians, then, must have entered marginal Polynesia carving their images in wood, and have fallen to fashioning them of easily worked tuff in Raivavai, Pitcairn, and Easter islands, and in the Marquesas. Only in the Marquesas did the Polynesian turn to basalt for carving copies of completely shaped human figures of wood.

The images, as well as oval-pointed bowls, considerably add to the likelihood of an ultimate southeastern origin of Necker Island culture, which the adzes clearly point out. The Necker type of marae, so prominent in southeast Polynesia, constitutes by itself almost complete proof of a southeast origin, for it, like the stone images, is totally lacking in Micronesia, and if present in central Polynesia is either disguised or undiscovered. It may be present in Melanesia; a low platform with uprights along the back is shown in illustrations of places of worship on Atchin Island, New Hebrides (37a).

In their uniformity, grouping, features, and arrangement of features the Necker maraes are remarkably similar to the maraes in the interior of Tahiti and the maraes of the western Tuamotus, and very dissimilar to Hawaiian and Marquesan religious structures. Yet elements of the Necker marae, more or less obscured, are preserved in a Kauai temple form. The inland Tahitian marae is an ancient form long in the process of being displaced by the coast marae, an elaboration and exaggeration of certain features of the older (16).

The squid-lure sinkers from Bowl Cave, like the Hawaiian type of adzes, determine that the Necker culture flowed by way of the main Hawaiian group, and not directly from the southeast, for these sinkers are, from their total absence elsewhere, a Hawaiian development. They bear, however, the mark of Necker individuality in their angular outline. An angular rendering of stone implements and utensils other than adzes is quite foreign to Hawaiian workmanship with the very significant exception of a class of archaic grinders or rubbers described by Stokes (44), from Kauai.

The key to Nihoa cultural relationships, like that of Necker, is furnished by the adzes. One adz is a typical Necker product; the other adzes are typically Hawaiian. The Necker stone vessels, the Necker style of stone working as illustrated by the coral rubber and the Necker marae are also represented on Nihoa, so the Necker pilgrims have there left clear evidence of themselves.

Plentiful among the remains on Nihoa are features purely of the historical Hawaiian culture, the most striking being the cupmortar. Nearly as convincing is the bone fishhook and the fisherman's shrines (*ko'a*). The tradition that Nihoa was known to the Hawaiians before the coming of the Europeans, printed 60 years ago by the historian Kamakau (27), is therefore well founded. Nihoa at one time supported a permanent population, which I estimate was not over 200. A problem not easily settled, is to whom to attribute the permanent population: to the people sharing the Necker culture, or to the historic Hawaiians?

As most of the twenty-five Nihoa stone vessels in the archaeological collection are of Necker types, it seems safe to attribute all the stone vessels to the Necker culture. The Nihoa vessels were picked up from all parts of the island, whereas the purely Hawaiian utensils and implements came only from five associated bluff-shelters in East Valley and from Site 41, in East Palm Valley. Hence, it is my conviction that the Necker people formed at least a fair size population and probably made up the permanent population which crowded the island with ruins. The stone vessels point to a period when the people of Nihoa were cut off from communication with the larger Hawaiian islands. This is explainable on the hypothesis that the people of the Necker cult were forced out of the main Hawaiian group and settled for a time on Nihoa. It is barely possible they were ousted from Nihoa by the historic Hawaiians, but it is more probable that long after the island had been abandoned by the Necker people, it was rediscovered by the Hawaiians and utilized as a seasonal camping ground for fishing or bird-hunting parties.

This review of the cultural affinities of Nihoa and Necker, reveals the Necker culture as one which had been introduced to the Hawaiian islands from southeast Polynesia, probably from Tahiti, and which, on the islands excepting Necker had become for the most part displaced, and for the rest, modified by the historic Hawaiian culture. Traces of the Necker culture are discernable on Nihoa, and to a slight extent on Kauai.

Necker Island obviously held a strong mystical attraction for the ancient Hawaiians, yet tradition is quite silent about it. In view of the large body of recorded historical traditions treating in some detail events from the thirteenth century onward, the muteness regarding Necker indicates that the island was not known or that it was early forgotten during the last seven centuries.

Though no traditions recognizably referring to Necker have survived, a good number, as Fornander (17a, pp. 46-58, and 17b, pp. 239-257) has admirably shown allude to a profound alteration of Hawaiian culture from a state which I believe identifiable with the Necker culture to the familiar Hawaiian, under the influence of immigrants from the Society Islands who came between 32 to 24 generations before 1900 (A. D. 1100 to 1300, allowing 25 years to a generation). These two centuries witnessed the sudden beginning and abrupt ending of a period of remarkable voyaging between the Hawaiian group and the islands to the south. From the close of this period to the appearance of the European no more is heard of adventurous navigators from southern islands: there is merely mention (17b, pp. 248, 249) of a few castaways between 19 and 15 generations ago (A. D. 1425-1525). The newcomers of the period of Tahitian influx, Fornander says (17b, pp. 252, 253), regarded Hawaii as a Kama na Tahiti (Child-of-Tahiti).

. . . a natural appanage of themselves, to be taken possession of and reconstructed by them and their posterity. . . . Whatever the condition in which they found the country, they moulded, reorganized, and arranged everything in their own pattern and, while they with most elaborate care have left us numerous momentoes of their own time and work, they have left us nearly none of their predecessors. . . .

I gather that they found the previous inhabitants of this group living in a primitive manner, without any political organization beyond the patriarchal, and without kapus—

at least any of a stringent naure—and without heiaus. . . . That is, heiaus of the rudest construction and most simple service. . . .

That the people of this [Hawaiian] group, whether chiefs or commoners, previous to this period [Tahitian immigration], were of Polynesian—or as they themselves called it— Tahitian origin, there is no good ground for doubting, and every reason to believe. But the time of their arrival and settlement, the mode of their arrival, their point of departure, and their political, religious, and social condition, will probably always remain insoluable problems.

That deliberate communication between the Hawaiian islands and the Society Islands occurred during the twelfth and thirteenth centuries, and that the changes mentioned by Fornander as having been wrought at that time were due to Society Island influences, present day comparative study of traditions and material culture make increasingly clear (17, 22, 26, 41, 42). However, the change in temple form described by Fornander (17a, pp. 6, 35, 36, 59, 60) as then having taken place was from some kind of open platform to a quadrangular walled enclosure such as the heiaus of Mookini and Wahaula on the island of Hawaii—heiaus said to have been established by the priest Paao, 28 generations ago. This was a change to a form akin to the coastal maraes of Tahiti and Moorea, and not to their older inland type of marae. Could it be that the Necker marae, so nearly identical to the inland Tahiti marae, appeared in Hawaii at the same period of Tahitian contact? Though the possibility can not be denied, considered against a background of Tahitian history it does not seem likely, inasmuch as the coastal maraes represent an element which had come into Tahiti from Raiatea by the twelfth and thirteenth centuries and which firmly imposed itself on the earlier culture and population represented in historic times by the inland marae and the lower class of people called the *manahune* (17; 22).

The Society Island immigrants whose names and exploits have been preserved in Hawaiian history certainly shared in full measure the ideas and institutions of the Raiatean families who were responsible for much the same cultural change in Tahiti as took place, although with far more sweeping effect, in the Hawaiian islands. It is hardly likely with the prominence and power they enjoyed in breaking in upon Hawaii's isolation, that they would have allowed the older Tahitian culture which they did not represent to have gained such a hold in the Hawaiian group as it evidently once had, if it came in during those years when they were vigorously shaping Hawaiian culture after their own pattern. It is more plausible, all things considered, that these exponents of the new culture emanating from Raiatea, found already established in Hawaii the maraes and culture they had long dealt with in Tahiti. Hence an explanation for the ease, rapidity, and completeness with which they effaced the earlier culture, weakened by its long seclusion. The notions which the Hawaiians seem to have preserved regarding the people living in Hawaii when the famous Tahitian voyagers appeared, were that these early occupants were Polynesians claiming to be from "Tahiti." They were regarded as a whole by the new arrivals as "a child of Tahiti" to be brought up according to the later enlightment of their homeland. The traditions imply that the early organization was simple in comparison with the later, and that the temples were simple, open platforms. All these conceptions are in perfect keeping with ancient Tahitian social organization and maraes, and with the relationships indicated by the Necker maraes. Therefore, unless or until evidence to the contrary is brought forth, it seems reasonable to adopt the view that the Necker culture is a pure sample of the culture prevailing in Hawaii before the thirteenth century, and that prehistoric as well as the historic Hawaiian culture may be considered Tahitian in origin.

LITERATURE CITED

1. ARAGO, J., Voyage autour du monde, Paris, 1825.
2. ATKINSON, A. L. C., Memorandum written August 8, 1923, immediately after an interview with Capt. Bruhn, manuscript, B. P. Bishop Museum.
3. BANKS, Journal of the Right Hon. Sir Joseph Banks, edited by Sir Joseph D. Hooker, London, 1896.
4. BEST, ELSDEN, The Maori, Wellington, 1924.
5. BEASLEY, H. G., Some Polynesian cuttlefish baits: Roy. Anthropological Inst. Great Britain and Ireland, Jour., vol. 51, pp. 100-114, 1921.
6. BISHOP, S. E., Nihoa, its topography, something about its geology. The trip in outline. Honolulu, 1885.
7. BISHOP, S. E., Geological and topographical report upon Nihoa, or Bird Island: The Hawaiian Government Survey, Honolulu, 1885.
7a. BUCK, P. H., Emory, K. P., Skinner, H. D., Stokes, J. F. G., Terminology for describing Polynesian adzes, manuscript in preparation.
8. CHUNG, H. L., Hawaiian Agricultural Experiment Station, Bull. 50, Honolulu, 1923.
9. COOK, JAMES, A voyage to the Pacific Ocean in the years 1776-1780 [third voyage], 3 vols. and atlas, London, 1784.
10. CORNEY, B. G., Quest and occupation of Tahiti: Hakluyt Soc., 2d ser., vol. 43, London, 1918.
11. CORNEY, PETER, Early North Pacific voyages, Honolulu, 1896.
12. DOLE, S. B., Proclamation of the annexation of Necker, June 12, 1894: Archives of Hawaii.
13. DOLE, S. B., Proclamation on annexation of Necker Island: Archives of Hawaii
13a. EDGE-PARTINGTON, JAMES, Album of weapons, tools, ornaments, and articles of dress, of the natives of the Pacific islands, Manchester, 1895.
14. ELLIS, S. W., Cook's last voyage, London, 1783.
15. ELSCHNER, C., The leeward islands of the Hawaiian group [Reprint from the Sunday Advertiser], Honolulu, 1915.
16. EMORY, K. P., Archaeology of the Society Islands: Soc. des Etudes Oceanienne, no. 12, pp. 29-33, 1926. Archaeology of the Society Islands, B. P. Bishop Museum, manuscript in preparation.
17. EMORY, K. P., Island of Lanai: B. P. Bishop Mus., Bull. 12, 1924.
17a. FORNANDER, ABRAHAM, The Polynesian race, vol. 2, London, 1878.
17b. FORNANDER, ABRAHAM, Fornander collection of antiquities and folk-lore: B. P. Bishop Mus., Mem., vol. 6, 1919-20.
18. THE FRIEND, monthly paper published by S. C. Damon, 1843-?, Honolulu.
18a. GREGORY, H. E., The geography of the Pacific: Problems of the Pacific, pp. 221-31, Chicago, 1928.
19. GREGORY, H. E., The Tanager Expedition: Report of the Director for 1923, B. P. Bishop Mus., Bull. 10, 1924.
20. GREGORY, H. E., The Tanager Expedition: Report of the Director for 1924, B. P. Bishop Mus., Bull. 21, 1925.
21. HANDY, E. S. C., Polynesian Religion: B. P. Bishop Mus., Bull. 34, 1927.
22. HANDY, E. S. C., Tahitian culture, B. P. Bishop Museum, manuscript in preparation.
23. HAWAIIAN CLUB papers, Boston, 1868.
24. HAWAIIAN GAZETTE, weekly newspaper published during the years 1865-?, Honolulu.
25. HAWAIIAN STAR, weekly newspaper published during the years 1893-1900 (?), Honolulu, combined with the Star-Bulletin.
26. HENRY, TEUIRA, Ancient Tahiti, B. P. Bishop Mus., Bull. 48, 1928.

27. KAMAKAU, S. M., Hawaiian history: Kuokoa, weekly newspaper in Hawaiian, Honolulu, Feb. 1, 1868.

28. KAMEHAMEHA IV, Instructions to Capt. John Paty: Interior Dept. bk. 6, p. 494a, 1857. (A written document.) Archives of Hawaii.

29. KING, J. A., Written report to President Dole. Archives of Hawaii.

30. LA PEROUSE, A voyage around the world, London, 1799.

31. LINTON, RALPH, The material culture of the Marquesas Islands: B. P. Bishop Mus., Mem., vol. 8, no. 5, 1923.

32. LINTON, RALPH, Archaeology of the Marquesas Islands: B. P. Bishop Mus., Bull. 23, 1925.

33. MARTIN, RUDOLF, Lehrbuch der Anthropologie, Jena, 1914.

34. MEARES, JOHN, Voyages in the years 1788 and 1789 from China to the northwest coast of America, London, 1790.

35. PACIFIC COMMERCIAL ADVERTISER, a daily paper, published during the years 1856-1894 (?), Honolulu.

36. PATY, JOHN, Journal of the voyage in the schooner Manuokawai in April and May, 1857, in both the original and the official log. In Archives of Hawaii (Extracts of the log are printed in the Polynesian, Honolulu, June 6, 1857, and in the Pacific Commercial Advertiser, Honolulu, June 11, 1857).

37. PALMER, H. S., Geology of Kaula, Nihoa, Necker, and Gardner islands: B. P. Bishop Mus., Bull. 35, 1927.

37a. PIGEON, HARRY, Around the world in the Islander: Nat. Geog. Mag., vol. 53, no. 2, February, 1928.

38. POLYNESIAN, THE, Weekly newspaper printed in English, during the years 1840-1863, Honolulu.

39. POSNASKY, A., Eine prehistorische metropole in Süd America, Berlin, 1914.

40. SEURAT, L. G., Les Marae des iles orientales de l'Archipel des Tuamotu; l'Anthropologie, vol. 16, 1905.

41. SMITH, S. PERCY, Hawaiki, London, 1921.

42. STOKES, J. F. G., The food rubbing stones of Kauai in connection with cultural diffusion in Hawaii, Hawaiian Academy of Sci., Proc. for 1927: B. P. Bishop Mus., Special Pub. 12, pp. 22-23, 1927.

43. STOKES, J. F. G., Whence Paao: Hawaiian Hist. Soc., Papers no. 15, pp. 40-45, 1928.

44. STOKES, J. F. G., Ethnology of Raivavai: B. P. Bishop Museum, manuscript in preparation.

45. STOKES, J. F. G., Walled fish traps of Pearl Harbor: B. P. Bishop Mus., Occ. Papers, vol. 4, no. 3, 1909.

46. THRUM, T. G., Editor, Hawaiian Annual for 1893, Honolulu, 1894.

47. THRUM, T. G., Editor, Hawaiian Annual for 1906, Honolulu, 1907.

48. THRUM, T. G., Editor, Hawaiian Annual for 1907, Honolulu, 1908.

49. WENTWORTH, C. K., Chink facetting: Jour. Geology, vol. 32, no. 3, pp. 260-267, 1925.

50. WENTWORTH, C. K., and PALMER, H. S., Eustatic bench of islands of the North Pacific: Geol. Soc. of Am., Bull. vol. 36, pp. 521-544, 1926.

51. WILSON, JAMES, Voyage to the South Pacific, London, 1799.

A

B

NIHOA ISLAND: *A*, THE ISLAND VIEWED FROM THE SOUTHEAST; *B*, TER-
RACE ON SEA CLIFF AT SITE 10, TWO UPRIGHT STONE SLABS IN LEFT REAR
CORNER, VIEWED FROM THE NORTHEAST.
(*A*, PHOTOGRAPH BY LIEUT. E. J. BROWN.)

A

B

WALL AND GROTTO, NIHOA ISLAND: *A*, WALL AT REAR OF PLATFORM ON
DOG HEAD, DIKE PRISMS AND CORAL HEADS ON WALL, VIEWED FROM THE
NORTH; *B*, GROTTO WITH TERRACED FLOOR AND WING WALLS AND A GARDEN
TERRACED TO THE RIGHT, SITE 19, VIEWED FROM THE EAST.

A

B

SHELTERS ON NIHOA ISLAND: *A*, STONE SHELTER, SITE 5, VIEWED FROM THE NORTH; *B*, BLUFF SHELTERS IN EAST VALLEY, SITES 56 TO 60, VIEWED FROM THE SOUTH.

(*A*, PHOTOGRAPH BY E. L. CAUM.)

B

A

TERRACES, NIHOA ISLAND: *A*, TERRACES IN MIDDLE VALLEY, REVEALED BY CLEARING, SITE 24 VIEWED FROM THE EAST (PL. VI, FOR NEAR VIEW); *B*, CENTRAL TERRACES SITE 40, VIEWED FROM THE WEST.

A

B

RETAINING WALLS, OF HOUSE TERRACES, NIHOA ISLAND: *A*, SITE 43, VIEWED FROM THE WEST; *B*, SIDE RETAINING WALL, SITE 36, VIEWED FROM THE NORTHEAST.

A

B

MARAES AND TERRACES, NIHOA ISLAND: *A*, THREE SETS OF AGRICULTURAL TERRACES AT SITE 24 (PL. IV, *A* SHOWS SITUATION); *B*, TWO ADJOINING MARAES AT SITE 50, UPRIGHT SLABS ON TERRACES, EXCAVATION OF LOWER MARAE IN PROGRESS; VIEWED FROM SOUTHEAST.

A

B

UPRIGHTS ON TERRACES, NIHOA ISLAND: *A*, AT SITE 41, LARGE COLUMN
ON RIGHT IS THAT NEAREST "4" ON THE PLAN FIGURE 10; *B*, AT REAR OF
FOURTH TERRACE, SITE 50 (PL. VI, *B*).

VIEWS OF NECKER ISLAND: *A*, NORTH COAST, VIEWED FROM ANNEXATION HILL; *B*, LANDING OF TANAGER EXPEDITION AT WEST CAVE, JUNE, 1923; *C*, ANNEXATION HILL AS VIEWED FROM FLAGPOLE HILL, LINES POINT TO MARAES AS LOCATED ON THE MAP, FIGURE 24. (THE NUMBER 3 SHOULD POINT TO THE SAME LOCATION AS 4, AS BOTH NUMBERS REFER TO THE SAME MARAE.)

A

B

SCENES ON NECKER ISLAND: *A*, MINISTER JAMES KING AT MARAE 1, READING PROCLAMATION OF ANNEXATION TO THE HAWAIIAN GOVERNMENT, MAY 27, 1897 (LEFT TO RIGHT—FIRST OFFICER, WILLIAM GREGORY, MINISTER JAMES KING, CAPTAIN FREEMAN, AND THREE SAILORS); *B*, VIEW LOOKING EASTWARD OVER SUMMITS FROM BOWL HILL, OCTOBER 9, 1919.

(*A*, PHOTOGRAPH BY B. H. NORTON.)

MARAES, NECKER ISLAND: *A*, UPRIGHTS AND PART OF PLATFORM OF MARAE 1, BOOBY PERCHED ON UPRIGHT NO. 7; *B*, MARAE 5, FROM THE SOUTHWEST; *C*, MARAE 18, FROM THE SOUTHEAST; *D*, MARAE 21, FROM THE NORTH.

A

B

MARAES, NECKER ISLAND: *A,* MARAE 24, FROM THE EAST; *B,* MARAE 31, FROM THE NORTH.

A

B

Marae and terraces, Necker Island: *A*, Marae 12 from the south-east; *B*, terraces "c" at site e, from the north.
(*A*, photograph by E. L. Caum.)

A

B

TERRACES, NECKER ISLAND: *A*, TWO TERRACES AT MARAE 29, FROM THE
NORTHEAST; *B*, LOWEST TERRACE AT SITE H, FROM THE SOUTH.

HEIAU IN WAIMEA VALLEY, KAUAI ISLAND, SHOWING DIKE PRISM UPRIGHT IN FOREGROUND AND ARRANGEMENT OF WOODEN SLABS NEAR ONE END.

(REPRODUCED FROM A DRAWING MADE BY J. WEBBER DURING THE LAST VOYAGE OF CAPTAIN COOK, 1778.)

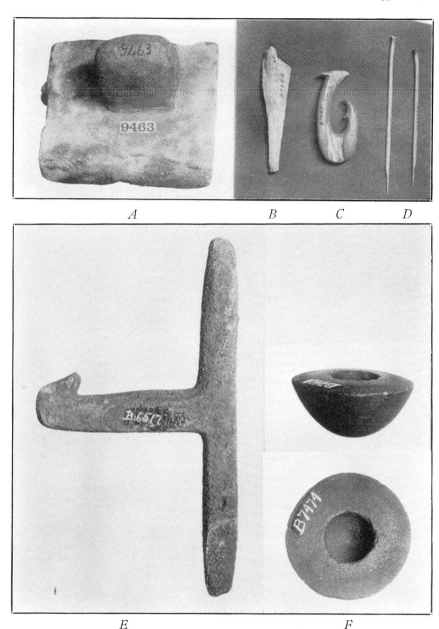

ARTIFACTS FROM NIHOA AND NECKER ISLANDS: A, CORAL RUBBING STONE
FROM NIHOA, COLLECTED BY MR. W. H. R. DEVERILL, IN 1885; B, HUMAN
BONE FROM WHICH A PIECE HAS BEEN CUT, LENGTH 3 INCHES, THICKNESS 8
INCHES NIHOA; C, FISHHOOK OF HUMAN BONE, NIHOA, MAXIMUM HEIGHT
2.2 INCHES, WIDTH 1.1 INCHES; D, TWO NEEDLES OF BIRD BONE, NIHOA; E,
BIRD-SNARING PERCH OF STONE, BOWL CAVE, NECKER: HEIGHT 9 INCHES,
WEIGHT 15 OUNCES; F, CUP MORTAR FROM SITE 41, NIHOA, TOP AND SIDE
VIEWS, HEIGHT 1.75 INCHES, DIAMETER 3.5 INCHES, DIAMETER OF CAVITY
1.25 INCHES, DEPTH OF CAVITY .8 INCHES, WEIGHT 13 OUNCES.

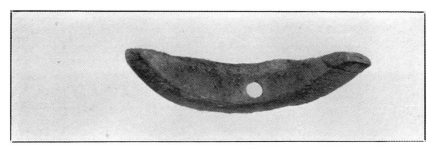

A

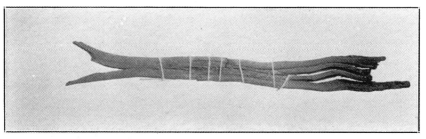

B

C

WOODEN OBJECTS FROM NIHOA ISLAND: *A*, SECTION OF RIM OF BOWL CUT TO MAKE A SCRAPER, FROM SITE 58, LENGTH 5 INCHES, THICKNESS .25 INCHES; *B*, NETTING SHUTTLE FROM SITE 58, LENGTH 7.5 INCHES; *C*, TILLER 31.5 INCHES LONG, MADE OF WOOD OF BREADFRUIT TREE, FROM SITE 66.

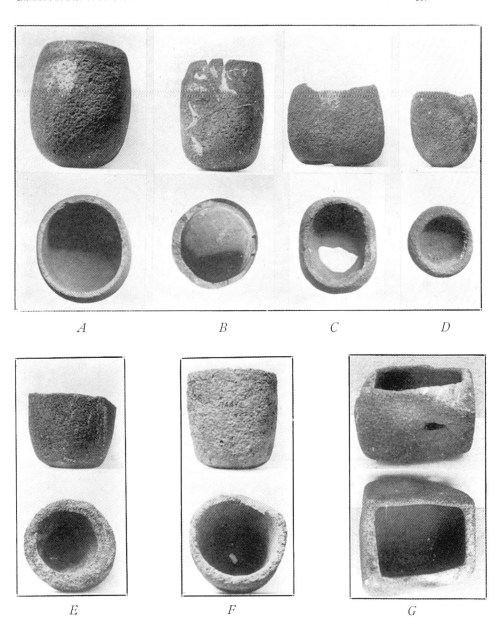

SIDE AND TOP VIEWS OF JARS AND POTS FROM NIHOA AND NECKER ISLANDS: *A*, JAR FROM SITE 7, NIHOA; *B*, JAR FROM SITE 66, NIHOA; *C*, JAR COLLECTED FROM NIHOA BY QUEEN LILIUOKALANI IN 1885; *D*, SHALLOWLY EXCAVATED JAR FROM SITE 41; *E*, POT FROM EAST PALM VALLEY, NIHOA; *F*, POT FROM EASTERN END OF NECKER ISLAND, COLLECTED IN 1894; *G*, RECTANGULAR BOWL FROM MIDDLE VALLEY, COLLECTED BY LIEUT. W. H. BAINBRIDGE, IN 1928.

A   *B*   *C*

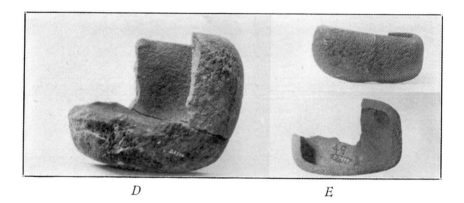

D   *E*

BOWLS FROM NIHOA ISLAND: *A*, FROM EAST PALM VALLEY, CAPACITY 72 OUNCES OF WATER; *B*, FROM SITE 41, CAPACITY 32 OUNCES; *C*, FROM SITE 40, 41, 42, OR 43; *D*, FROM SITE 48; *E*, DISH OR LOW BOWL FROM SITE 41.

A   *B*   *C*   *D*

E   *F*   *G*

DISHES, BOWLS, AND STONE OBJECTS FROM NIHOA AND NECKER ISLANDS: *A*, DISH FROM NIHOA, 8 INCHES LONG, 5.5 INCHES WIDE, 4 INCHES HIGH, COLLECTED IN 1885; *B*, DISH FROM BOWL CAVE, NECKER, TOP VIEW, 13.5 INCHES LONG, 7.5 INCHES WIDE, 3.25 INCHES HIGH; *C*, RESHAPED ARM OF IMAGE FROM NEAR MARAE 12, NECKER; *D*, GROOVED STONE FROM NEAR MARAE 12, NECKER; *E*, OVAL POINTED BOWL IN THE ROUGH, FROM BOWL HILL, NECKER; *F*, FINISHED OVAL POINTED BOWL FROM BOWL CAVE, NECKER; *G*, GROOVED STONE FROM SITE 41, WEIGHT 13 POUNDS, NIHOA.

A

B

STONE IMAGES FROM NECKER ISLAND: *A*, FIVE OF THE SEVEN IMAGES
COLLECTED BY THE ANNEXATION PARTY OF MAY, 1894, THE SECOND AND
FOURTH IMAGES, COUNTING FROM THE LEFT, HAVE BECOME LOST, THE SECOND
IMAGE IS 8.3 INCHES HIGH (THE HEAD ALONE, 5.4 INCHES) AND WHEN
COMPLETE WAS PROBABLY 10 INCHES HIGH, THE FOURTH IMAGE IS 5 INCHES
HIGH; *B*, IMAGE NOW LOST, COLLECTED BY OFFICER OF THE CHAMPION IN
1894, FORMERLY IN POSSESSION OF THE ATKINSON FAMILY.

(*A*, PHOTOGRAPH BY WEATHERWAX IN 1894.)

A   B   C   D

FRONT, PROFILE, AND BACK VIEWS OF STONE IMAGES FROM MARAE 12, NECKER ISLAND: *A*, HEIGHT 15 INCHES (HEAD 6 INCHES), WEIGHT 25 POUNDS; *B*, HEIGHT 16.1 INCHES (HEAD 6.4 INCHES), WEIGHT 22.5 POUNDS; *C*, HEIGHT 14.9 INCHES (HEAD 4.3 INCHES), WEIGHT 14 POUNDS; *D*, HEIGHT 15.1 INCHES (HEAD 4.3 INCHES), WEIGHT 14.75 POUNDS. (IN BERNICE P. BISHOP MUSEUM.)

A   B

FRONT, PROFILE, AND BACK VIEWS OF TWO STONE IMAGES FROM NECKER
ISLAND, COLLECTED BY OFFICERS OF THE H. M. S. CHAMPION IN 1894, FROM
MARAE 12; A, HEIGHT 19 INCHES; B, HEIGHT 11.5 INCHES.
(IN BRITISH MUSEUM.)

A   B   C

D   D   F

STONE IMAGES FROM NECKER ISLAND: *A*, RESHAPED, HEADLESS, ARMLESS IMAGE, FOUND BY GERRIT P. WILDER IN 1919 NEAR MARAE 1, HEIGHT 7.5 INCHES, WEIGHT 2.5 POUNDS; *B*, IMAGE HEAD COLLECTED BY OFFICERS OF THE CHAMPION IN 1894, HEIGHT 4 INCHES, WEIGHT 3 POUNDS; LEG FOUND BY GERRIT P. WILDER IN 1919 NEAR MARAE 12, LENGTH 4 INCHES, WEIGHT 1.5 POUNDS; *C*, IMAGE PRESENTED BY HON. SANFORD B. DOLE AND PRESUMABLY COLLECTED BY THE ANNEXATION PARTY, HEIGHT 7.5 INCHES; *D-F*, FRONT, RIGHT SIDE, AND BACK VIEWS OF UNFINISHED IMAGE FOUND AT MARAE 12 BY CHARLES S. JUDD IN 1923, HEIGHT 11.5 INCHES.